I0411881

July 2014

EDUCATION OF HOMELESS STUDENTS

Improved Program Oversight Needed

GAO-14-465

Highlights

Highlights of GAO-14-465, a report to congressional requesters

EDUCATION OF HOMELESS STUDENTS

Improved Program Oversight Needed

Why GAO Did This Study

The McKinney-Vento Homeless Assistance Act established a grant program to help the nation's homeless students—more than one million in school year 2011-12—have access to public education. Under the Education for Homeless Children and Youth grant program, states and their school districts are required to identify homeless children and provide them with needed services and support. In fiscal year 2014, Education received about $65 million to administer this program. Education provided formula grants to states, which competitively awarded funds to school districts to help meet program requirements. GAO was asked to review program implementation and oversight.

GAO examined (1) how districts identify and serve homeless students and challenges they face (2) how Education and states collaborate with other service providers to address student needs and any barriers, and (3) the extent to which Education monitors program compliance. GAO reviewed relevant federal laws, guidance, and reports, and analyzed Education's state and school district survey data from school year 2010-11. GAO also interviewed federal officials, and state and local officials in 20 school districts—representing a mix of urban, suburban, and rural districts and grant status—in four states, selected for geographic diversity and other characteristics, such as experience with natural disasters.

What GAO Recommends

GAO recommends that Education develop a plan to ensure adequate oversight of the EHCY program. Education concurred with our recommendation.

View GAO-14-465. For more information, contact Kay Brown at (202) 512-7215 or brownke@gao.gov.

What GAO Found

To identify and serve homeless students under the Education for Homeless Children and Youth (EHCY) program, officials in the 20 school districts where GAO conducted interviews reported conducting a range of activities to support homeless youth, but cited several challenges. With regard to GAO's interviews, 13 of the 20 districts identified homeless students through housing surveys at enrollment, while all 20 relied on referrals from schools or service providers. However, officials in 8 of the 20 districts noted that the under-identification of homeless students was a problem. Districts GAO reviewed provided eligible students with transportation to and from school, educational services, and referrals to other service providers for support such as health care or food assistance. Among the challenges that officials in the 20 districts cited were limited staff and resources to provide services, the cost of transportation, student stigma associated with homelessness, and responding to students made homeless by natural disasters. Nationally, school districts surveyed most recently in school year 2010-11 by the Department of Education (Education) reported providing many services while facing similar challenges.

Education's EHCY program manager and state program coordinators have collaborated with other government agencies and with private organizations by sharing information, participating in interagency councils on homelessness, and providing technical assistance to relevant staff. In addition, state EHCY program coordinators have provided training to school districts and helped connect local programs to ensure homeless students receive various services. However, federal and state officials frequently cited limited resources and differing federal definitions of homelessness as constraints to greater collaboration.

Education has protocols for monitoring state EHCY programs, but no plan to ensure adequate oversight of all states, though monitoring is a key management tool for assessing the quality of performance over time and resolving problems promptly. Prior to fiscal year 2010, it had been Education's policy to monitor 50 states and 3 area programs at least once during a 3-year period, and it did so for fiscal years 2007 to 2009. Subsequently, the department adopted a risk-based approach in fiscal year 2010 and monitored 28 states over the next 3 years. In fiscal year 2013, Education again changed its approach to EHCY program monitoring and has monitored 3 state programs since then. Department officials cited other priorities and a lack of staff capacity as reasons for the decrease in oversight. As a result, Education lacks assurance that states are complying with program requirements. GAO found gaps in state monitoring of districts that could weaken program performance, reinforcing the importance of effective federal monitoring of states.

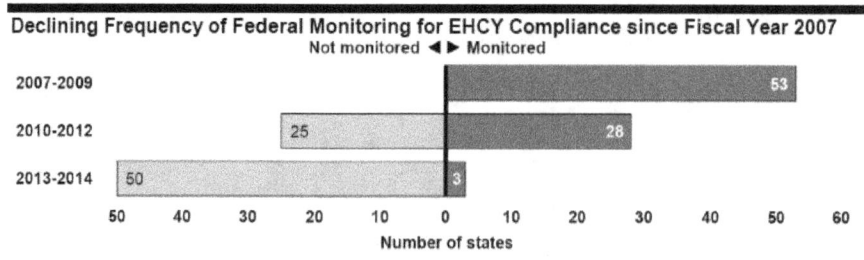

Declining Frequency of Federal Monitoring for EHCY Compliance since Fiscal Year 2007

Not monitored ◀ ▶ Monitored

	Not monitored	Monitored
2007-2009		53
2010-2012	25	28
2013-2014	50	3

Number of states

Source: GAO analysis of Department of Education documents. | GAO-14-465

Contents

Tables

Figures

Abbreviations

21st CCLC	21st Century Community Learning Centers
CoC	Continuum of Care
Education	Department of Education
EHCY	Education for Homeless Children and Youth
ESEA	Elementary and Secondary Education Act of 1965, as amended
HHS	Department of Health and Human Services
HUD	Department of Housing and Urban Development
LEA	Local Educational Agency
LGBTQ	Lesbian, Gay, Bisexual, Transgender, or Questioning
MEP	Migrant Education Program
NAEHCY	National Association for the Education of Homeless Children and Youth
NCHE	National Center for Homeless Education
RHY	Runaway and Homeless Youth programs
SASA	Student Achievement and School Accountability
SEA	State Educational Agency
USICH	United States Interagency Council on Homelessness

GAO U.S. GOVERNMENT ACCOUNTABILITY OFFICE

441 G St. N.W.
Washington, DC 20548

July 31, 2014

The Honorable Tom Harkin
Chairman
Committee on Health, Education, Labor, and Pensions
United States Senate

The Honorable Patty Murray
United States Senate

In school year 2011-12, more than 1.1 million children and youth enrolled in our nation's public schools were identified as homeless, according to data from the U.S. Department of Education (Education).[1] Homeless children and youth may face a variety of barriers to continuing their education, including frequent moves, a lack of transportation to and from school, and a lack of adequate supplies and services, such as counseling, that may be necessary to help them remain in school. Research on homeless and highly mobile children suggests that they face challenges with academic achievement and school completion. We previously reported that students who change schools more frequently tend to have lower scores on standardized reading and math tests and drop out of school at higher rates than their less mobile peers.[2] In addition, according to a study of an urban school district from school years 2005-06 to 2009-10, homeless and highly mobile children were more likely to exhibit lower levels of academic achievement compared with other students.[3]

The Education for Homeless Children and Youth (EHCY) program, initially authorized by Title VII-B of the McKinney-Vento Homeless Assistance Act (McKinney-Vento Act), helps address barriers to school

---

[1]Department of Education, National Center for Homeless Education, *Education for Homeless Children and Youths Program: Data Collection Summary* (March 2014).

[2]GAO, K-12 *Education: Many Challenges Arise in Educating Students Who Change Schools Frequently*, GAO-11-40 (Washington, D.C.: Nov. 18, 2010).

[3]J. J. Cutuli et al., "Academic Achievement Trajectories of Homeless and Highly Mobile Students: Resilience in the Context of Chronic and Acute Risk," *Child Development*, vol. 84, no. 3 (2013).

enrollment, attendance, and success for homeless children and youth.[4] The act requires state educational agencies to ensure that homeless children and youth have equal access to the same free appropriate public education, including a public preschool education, as provided to other children. Congress appropriated about $65 million to carry out the EHCY program in fiscal year 2014.[5] The McKinney-Vento Act authorizes Education to provide federal grants to states to administer and oversee activities under the EHCY program.[6] In turn, states award a majority of these funds on a competitive basis to select school districts in their state (grantee districts), based on factors such as the needs of homeless children and youth within a particular district and the ability of the district to meet those needs.[7] Regardless of whether a school district receives EHCY program funds, all districts must comply with certain program requirements, which include ensuring that homeless children and youth are appropriately identified, immediately enrolled in school, and receive the educational and other services for which they are eligible, such as transportation to and from school. In addition, as GAO has reported in the past, collaboration presents an opportunity to increase the efficiency and effectiveness of federal programs.[8] Because no one system of services can meet every need of students experiencing homelessness, and

---

[4]Stewart B. McKinney Homeless Assistance Act, Pub. L. No. 100-77, §§ 721-725, 101 Stat. 482, 525-28 (codified as amended at 42 U.S.C. §§ 11431-11435). In 2000, the law was renamed the McKinney-Vento Homeless Assistance Act. Pub. L. No. 106-400, 114 Stat. 1675 (2000). The EHCY program was significantly amended by the McKinney-Vento Homeless Education Assistance Improvements Act of 2001, enacted as part of the No Child Left Behind Act of 2001, Pub. L. No. 107-110, §§ 1031-1034, 115 Stat. 1425, 1989-2007 (2002).

[5]See generally Consolidated Appropriations Act, 2014, Pub. L. No. 113-76, div. H, tit. III, 128 Stat. 5, 391-92 (2013). The amount for the EHCY program was specified in a report from the Senate Committee on Appropriations. S. Rep. No. 113-71, at 166 (2013).

[6]See 42 U.S.C. § 11432. In general, subject to minimum award requirements, the amount that a state receives for the EHCY program is based on the proportion of funds allocated nationally that it receives under Title I, Part A of the Elementary and Secondary Education Act of 1965, as amended (ESEA).

[7]See 42 U.S.C. § 11433. For purposes of this report, we use the term "school district" to refer to a local educational agency. In addition, for the purposes of our report, we refer to districts that received an EHCY grant from their state as "grantee districts," and those that did not as "non-grantee districts."

[8]GAO, *2013 Annual Report: Actions Needed to Reduce Fragmentation, Overlap, and Duplication and Achieve Other Financial Benefits*, GAO-13-279SP (Washington, D.C.: Apr. 9, 2013).

funding for the EHCY program is set at relatively modest levels, collaboration at the federal, state, and local levels is essential to address the academic and non-academic needs of homeless students. The McKinney-Vento Act requires states and school districts to coordinate and collaborate with other programs and service providers that also serve these children and youth. In light of the issues facing homeless students, you asked us to examine the implementation and oversight of the EHCY program.

This report addresses (1) how school districts identify and serve homeless students and the challenges in doing so, (2) how Education and states collaborate with other agencies and service providers to address the needs of homeless students and barriers to collaboration, and (3) the extent to which Education monitors compliance with the EHCY program requirements and how Education assesses program results.

To gather information on how the EHCY program is implemented at the local level, we visited three states—Colorado, New Jersey, and Washington—and interviewed officials in Texas by phone.[9] We selected states that represent geographic diversity and based on the recommendations of experts, including the National Association for the Education of Homeless Children and Youth (NAEHCY)[10] and other national organizations working on issues related to homelessness, to obtain a mix of states implementing promising practices in their EHCY programs as well as experiencing challenges. In addition, we sought variation in the number of homeless students states identified in recent years and the size of states' EHCY grants, among other factors. We also selected two states that have recently experienced natural disasters to see how they coped with sudden increases in the number of homeless students. In each state, we interviewed state and school district officials. In total, we spoke with school district officials from 20 different school districts, nine of which were grantee districts. We selected these districts

---

[9]It was not the purpose of this report to assess states' or districts' compliance with the McKinney-Vento Act.

[10]NAEHCY is a membership organization made up of local homeless education liaisons, educators, school counselors, social workers, registrars, nurses, child advocates, shelter staff, state and federal policy specialists, and partners from community-based and national non-profit organizations. It provides professional development, resources, and training support on meeting the educational needs of children and youth experiencing homelessness.

GAO-14-465 Education of Homeless Students

with the assistance of state EHCY program coordinators to represent a mix of urban, suburban, and rural districts, as well as grantee and non-grantee districts. In the states we visited, we also met with school officials and youth or their families who have experienced homelessness. Information obtained from these states and school districts is non-generalizable. To obtain generalizable and national-level information on states and grantee school districts, we analyzed Education data from two surveys covering school year 2010-11, which we found to be sufficiently reliable.[11] We assessed the reliability of the survey data by performing electronic testing of the data elements, reviewing relevant documentation, and interviewing agency officials knowledgeable about the data. We used the survey data to examine how states and school districts implement the EHCY program and how states monitor school districts, among other things. All estimates obtained from the school district-level survey have margins of error of no greater than six percentage points. To obtain information on how Education administers the EHCY program and collaborates with other agencies, we interviewed Education officials and officials from other federal agencies, including the Departments of Health and Human Services (HHS) and Housing and Urban Development (HUD), as well as the U.S. Interagency Council on Homelessness (USICH). We also reviewed relevant documents—including federal laws and regulations, monitoring protocols, and policy memos—and examined Education's findings on the EHCY program from state monitoring reports. See appendix I for additional information on our scope and methodology.

We conducted this performance audit from July 2012 through July 2014 in accordance with generally accepted government auditing standards. Those standards require that we plan and perform the audit to obtain sufficient, appropriate evidence to provide a reasonable basis for our findings and conclusions based on our audit objectives. We believe that the evidence obtained provides a reasonable basis for our findings and conclusions based on our audit objectives.

---

[11]Education is expected to release a report based on these surveys in 2014.

Background

The Education for Homeless Children and Youth Program

The EHCY program is the key federal education program targeted to homeless children and youth, and, in school year 2011-12, more than 1.1 million were enrolled in our nation's public schools,[12] according to Education data.[13] For purposes of the program, a homeless child or youth is one who lacks a fixed, regular, and adequate nighttime residence. This includes children who:

- are sharing the housing of others due to loss of housing, economic hardship, or a similar reason (commonly referred to as "doubled-up");
- are living in motels, hotels, trailer parks, or camping grounds due to the lack of alternative adequate accommodations;
- are living in emergency or transitional shelters; are abandoned in hospitals; or are awaiting foster care placement;
- have a primary nighttime residence that is a public or private place not designed for or ordinarily used as a regular sleeping accommodation for human beings;
- are living in cars, parks, public spaces, abandoned buildings, substandard housing, bus or train stations, or similar settings; and
- are migratory children who qualify as homeless due to their living circumstances, as described above.[14]

Education's Office of Student Achievement and School Accountability (SASA)—within the Office of Elementary and Secondary Education— provides EHCY formula grants to states, which must comply with certain

---

[12]These data include only those children and youth enrolled in school who were identified and reported as homeless by school districts; these data do not include homeless children and youth enrolled in school who were not identified or reported by school districts or homeless children and youth not enrolled in school. Due to changes in how the data collection instrument for states was pre-populated beginning in school year 2011-12, the number of homeless students that year cannot be compared to prior years. However, Education reported a 13 percent increase in the number of homeless students enrolled— from 939,903 to 1,065,794—between school years 2009-10 and 2010-11.

[13]Department of Education, National Center for Homeless Education, *Education for Homeless Children and Youths Program: Data Collection Summary* (March 2014).

[14]42 U.S.C. § 11434a(2). In this report, when we refer to the EHCY program definition of homelessness, we mean this definition. "Migratory child" is defined in section 1309 of the ESEA, see 20 U.S.C. § 6399(2).

requirements.[15] For example, the McKinney-Vento Act requires each state that receives funds to establish an Office of Coordinator for Education of Homeless Children and Youths, with responsibilities that include carrying out the state plan.[16] The state plan describes, among other things, procedures that will be used to identify homeless children and youth, strategies to address challenges, such as enrollment delays, and a demonstration of the state's efforts to review and revise policies to remove barriers to the enrollment and retention of homeless children and youth. Among other responsibilities, state educational agencies report data to Education on the educational needs of their homeless students; provide technical assistance to school districts and monitor their compliance with the program; and facilitate collaboration between the state and other service providers that serve homeless children and youth and their families.

States are generally required to award no less than 75 percent of their grant to school districts on a competitive basis.[17] Grants to school districts, awarded for a period of up to 3 years, are to be used for activities that facilitate the enrollment, attendance, and success of homeless children and youth in school. Grants to districts are to be awarded based on the need of the school district for assistance and the quality of the application submitted.[18] In determining which districts to fund, states are required to consider certain factors, such as the needs of homeless children and youth enrolled in the school district, the types of services to be provided under the program, and the extent to which the services will be coordinated with other services available to homeless children and youth. Districts are authorized to use these funds to support a range of activities for homeless students, such as tutoring, transportation, and referrals to health care services, as well as to provide

---

[15]See generally 42 U.S.C. § 11432. In addition to the 50 states, the District of Columbia, Puerto Rico, the outlying areas (the U.S. Virgin Islands, Guam, American Samoa, and the Northern Mariana Islands) and the Bureau of Indian Affairs also receive funds. Apart from the outlying areas and the Bureau of Indian Affairs, funds are generally allocated to states based on each state's share of ESEA Title I, Part A funds.

[16] For the purposes of this report, we refer to the Office of Coordinator as the state coordinator for the EHCY program.

[17]42 U.S.C. §§ 11432(e)(1), 11433(c)(1). States that receive the minimum state award amount are required to distribute no less than 50 percent to districts. States may use the remaining funds for state-level activities.

[18]42 U.S.C. § 11433(c).

professional development for educators and support coordination between schools and other agencies.[19] According to Education data, in school year 2011-12, fewer than a quarter of school districts nationwide (3,531 out of 16,064) received EHCY program funds; these districts enrolled 68 percent of the homeless students identified that year.[20]

Education also allows states to use a regional approach to award their competitive grants. Through such an approach, according to the National Center for Homeless Education (NCHE),[21] a state may provide funds to established regional educational entities, geographic clusters of school districts defined by the state, clusters self-selected by neighboring school districts, or some combination of these approaches. According to Education's survey of states in school year 2010-11, the most recent survey data available, 16 states reported that they provided funds through an intermediate educational agency or consortia.

Regardless of whether a school district receives EHCY program funds, all school districts are required to comply with certain requirements of the McKinney-Vento Act, including designating a homeless liaison to ensure that homeless children and youth are appropriately identified and provided the educational services for which they are eligible, among other things.[22] Under the McKinney-Vento Act, homeless children and youth have certain rights, including the right to:

- remain in their school of origin, if in their best interest;[23]

---

[19]42 U.S.C. § 11433(d).

[20]Data from school year 2011-12 are the most recent data available.

[21]NCHE is Education's technical assistance and information center for the EHCY program. It provides research, resources, and information that help communities address the educational needs of children experiencing homelessness. NCHE also supports educators and service providers by producing training and awareness materials, and providing training at regional and national conferences and events.

[22]42 U.S.C. § 11432(g)(1)(J)(ii), (g)(6).

[23]The "school of origin" is the school that the child or youth attended when permanently housed or the school in which the child or youth was last enrolled. 42 U.S.C. § 11432(g)(3)(G). In determining the best interest of a child or youth, a district must, to the extent feasible, keep a homeless child or youth in the school of origin unless doing so is contrary to the wishes of the child or youth's parent or guardian. 42 U.S.C. § 11432(g)(3)(A)-(B).

- immediately enroll in the selected school, even without the records, such as proof of residency, typically required;[24] and
- receive services comparable to those offered to other students for which they are eligible, such as transportation, educational services, and free school meals.[25]

Other Federal Programs that May Also Support Homeless Children and Youth

Other programs administered by Education and other federal agencies, many of which receive more federal funding than the EHCY program, may also support the needs of homeless children and youth (see table 1 for selected examples). For example, under Title I, Part A of the Elementary and Secondary Education Act of 1965, as amended (ESEA), school districts are required to set aside funds as necessary to provide comparable services for homeless students who do not attend Title I schools.[26] In addition, grantee school districts are required to coordinate with other organizations serving homeless children and youth, including those operating programs funded under the Runaway and Homeless Youth Act.[27] The populations served by these programs vary, and for some programs, eligibility for services does not depend on being homeless. Among the programs that do target homeless populations, some use definitions of homelessness that are different from the one used by the EHCY program.[28]

---

[24] 42 U.S.C. § 11432(g)(3)(C).

[25] 42 U.S.C. § 11432(g)(4).

[26] 20 U.S.C. § 6313(c)(3)(A). Under Education's regulations, school districts are also directed to reserve Title I funds as reasonable and necessary to conduct "other authorized activities," which, according to Education officials, could include providing additional support to homeless students who do attend Title I schools. 34 C.F.R. § 200.77(g). In addition, the Consolidated Appropriations Act, 2014 authorized school districts to use Title I funds to support homeless liaisons and provide transportation for homeless students to their schools of origin. Education notified state Title I directors and EHCY state coordinators of these new flexibilities in a letter dated March 21, 2014.

[27] 42 U.S.C. § 11432(g)(5). Runaway and Homeless Youth programs provide temporary emergency shelter, transitional housing, street outreach services, and maternity group home programs for youths to help them transition to self-sufficiency.

[28] For example, a different provision in the McKinney-Vento Act defines homeless individuals eligible for services under the Homeless Assistance programs administered by HUD. See 42 U.S.C. § 11302. Other programs, such as the Head Start program administered by HHS, use the EHCY definition of homeless children and youth. 42 U.S.C. § 9832(11).

Table 1: Examples of Federal Programs that May Also Serve Homeless Children and Youth

Federal Agency	Program	Description	Funding for fiscal year 2014 (in millions of dollars)
Education	Improving Basic Programs Operated by Local Educational Agencies (Title I, Part A of the Elementary and Secondary Education Act)	Provides financial assistance to school districts and schools with high concentrations of children from low-income families to help ensure that all children meet challenging state academic standards	14, 384.8
Education	Individuals with Disabilities Education Act, Parts B and C	Part B supports special education and related services for children with disabilities aged 3–21 and Part C supports early intervention services for children younger than 3 years of age	12,264.6
Education	Migrant Education Program	Aims to ensure that migratory children are provided with appropriate education services that address their special needs and receive full and appropriate opportunities to meet the same challenging state academic content and student academic achievement standards that all children are expected to meet, among other purposes	374.8
Education	21st Century Community Learning Centers	Supports the creation of community learning centers that provide academic enrichment opportunities during non-school hours for children, particularly students who attend high-poverty and low-performing schools	1,149.4
HHS	Head Start	Serves preschool-age children and their families and promotes the school readiness of children from birth to age 5 from low-income families by enhancing their cognitive, social, and emotional development[a]	8,598.1
HHS	Runaway and Homeless Youth	Supports temporary emergency shelter, transitional housing, street outreach services, and maternity group home programs to serve and protect runaway and homeless youth	114.1
HUD	Homeless Assistance Programs (including Emergency Solutions Grants and Continuum of Care Program)	Provide emergency shelter, supportive services, transitional housing, permanent housing, and prevention resources to assist individuals in shelters or on the streets attain permanent housing and self-sufficiency	2,105.0

Source: Education, HHS, and HUD agency program descriptions and budget documents for fiscal year 2015, reporting appropriated amounts for fiscal year 2014. | GAO-14-465

Note: This table is not intended to be exhaustive; other programs may also serve homeless children and youth that are not descr bed here.
[a]Homeless children are automatically eligible for the Head Start program.

The McKinney-Vento Act also created the U.S. Interagency Council on Homelessness (USICH), which currently consists of 19 federal cabinet secretaries and agency heads.[29] The Homeless Emergency Assistance and Rapid Transition to Housing (HEARTH) Act of 2009 established as the mission of USICH to coordinate the federal response to homelessness and create a national partnership at every level of government and with the private sector to reduce and end homelessness.[30]

Selected School Districts Leveraged Existing Resources to Identify and Serve Homeless Students, but Faced Resource Limitations and Other Challenges

Selected School Districts Largely Relied on Enrollment Forms and Referrals to Identify Homeless Students, but Faced Challenges and Noted Problems with Under-Identification

To identify homeless students, officials in a majority of school districts (13 of 20) said their districts systematically requested some information on the housing status of new students using a form during the enrollment process.[31] Two of these districts also requested housing information from every student every year to help identify eligible students whose housing circumstances may have changed following enrollment. According to the National Center for Homeless Education (NCHE), using a questionnaire at enrollment can help school districts increase their identification of homeless students (see fig. 1).

[29]See 42 U.S.C. §§ 11311-11320. Title II of the McKinney-Vento Act established the "Interagency Council on the Homeless" in 1987. The Consolidated Appropriations Act, 2004, renamed it the "United States Interagency Council on Homelessness." Pub. L. No. 108-199, div. G, § 216, 118 Stat. 3, 394.

[30]Pub. L. No. 111-22, div. B, § 1004, 123 Stat. 1632, 1666 (codified at 42 U.S.C. § 11311).

[31]Officials in the remaining seven districts told us they used other methods to identify homeless students. For example, districts may identify students as homeless informally at enrollment through conversations with new students.

Figure 1: Excerpt of Possible Housing Situations from an Example of an Education for Homeless Children and Youth Eligibility Determination Form

Please choose which of the following situations the student currently resides in (you can choose more than one):

_____ House or apartment with parent or guardian

_____ Motel, car, or campsite

_____ Shelter or other temporary housing

_____ With friends or family members (other than or in addition to parent/guardian)

If you are living in shared housing, please check all of the following reasons that apply:

_____ Loss of housing

_____ Economic situation

_____ Temporarily waiting for house or apartment

_____ Provide care for a family member

_____ Living with boyfriend/girlfriend

_____ Loss of employment

_____ Parent/Guardian is deployed

_____ Other (Please explain)

Are you a student under the age of 18 and living apart from your parents or guardians? Yes No

Source: National Center for Homeless Education. | GAO-14-465

To identify students who were not identified at enrollment or whose housing status changed during the year, homeless liaisons in the 20 school districts we interviewed also relied on referrals from school staff or other service providers (see fig. 2).[32]

---

[32]Under the McKinney-Vento Act, liaisons are to ensure that homeless students are identified by school personnel and through coordination with other entities and agencies. 42 U.S.C. § 11432(g)(6)(A)(i).

Figure 2: Examples of Referral Sources for Homeless Students

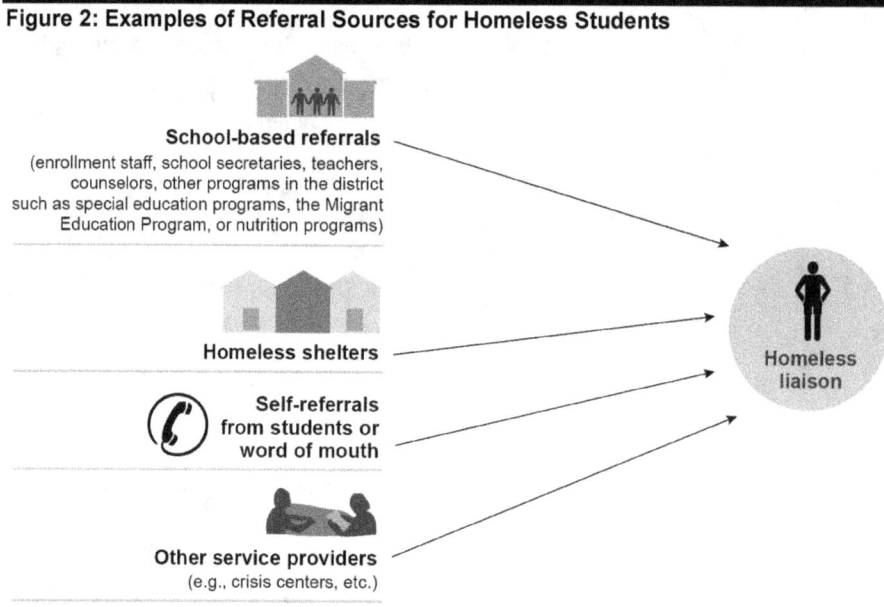

School-based referrals
(enrollment staff, school secretaries, teachers, counselors, other programs in the district such as special education programs, the Migrant Education Program, or nutrition programs)

Homeless shelters

Self-referrals from students or word of mouth

Other service providers
(e.g., crisis centers, etc.)

Homeless liaison

Source: GAO analysis of interviews with district officials. | GAO-14-465

Officials said they provided information and training to a variety of staff in contact with students to help them recognize potential signs of homelessness, such as:

- students who provide home addresses of shelters or other students;
- students who request transportation changes;
- students with attendance problems or who are tardy;
- students who fall asleep in class; and
- students with dropping grades, hunger, or hygiene issues.

Officials we interviewed also discussed the importance of training staff to identify homeless students, as identifying currently enrolled students is less systematic than identifying new students at enrollment.

Despite ongoing efforts to identify homeless students through housing surveys and referrals, officials in 8 out of the 20 districts we interviewed noted a problem with the under-identification of homeless students. All four state EHCY program coordinators we interviewed acknowledged that school districts face financial disincentives to identifying homeless children and youth due to the cost of services districts must provide.

Officials from both grantee and non-grantee districts[33] reported facing significant challenges in identifying all eligible students.[34]

Student Mobility

Officials in 11 of the 20 districts we interviewed said they identified increasing numbers of homeless children and youth in recent years, and many noted the frequent mobility of some students, making it challenging for school staff to keep track of their homeless students.

Confusion Regarding Applying Eligibility Requirements

Officials in 4 of the 20 districts said it was challenging to identify children and youth living doubled-up with others, particularly where living with extended family may be a cultural norm. In such cases, families may not consider themselves to be homeless or may be unaware of their rights to receive services under the program. For example, officials in one district told us that many of the district's immigrant families who work for a local meat processor live with relatives in doubled-up conditions but do not consider themselves homeless. To help clarify program eligibility, one district we reviewed used its enrollment form to ask parents or guardians to check a box when they are "living 'doubled-up' due to economic emergency, not to save money or for cultural preference."

Limited Information from Housing Surveys

In one school district we reviewed, the enrollment form asks parents or guardians to check a box "if the student is homeless or living in temporary/transitional housing," and asks whether the student is an "unaccompanied youth," but does not describe eligible housing situations. As a result, a student who is living doubled-up due to economic circumstances may not be identified, even though this situation represents a majority of homeless students nationwide (see fig. 3).

---

[33]For the purposes of our report, we will refer to districts that received an EHCY grant from their state as "grantee districts," and those that did not as "non-grantee districts."

[34]Three of four state EHCY program coordinators we interviewed said grantee and non-grantee districts generally face the same challenges. The fourth state EHCY program coordinator did not compare challenges between grantee and non-grantee districts.

Figure 3: Percent of Homeless Students Enrolled Nationwide by Primary Nighttime Residence, School Year 2011-12

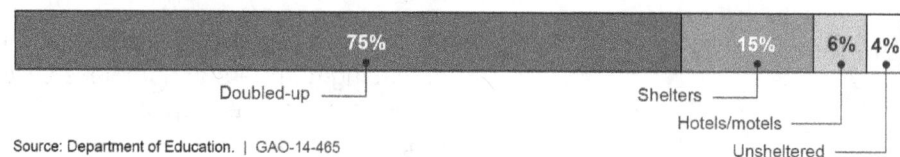

| 75% | 15% | 6% | 4% |

Doubled-up ———
Shelters ———
Hotels/motels ———
Unsheltered ———

Source: Department of Education. | GAO-14-465

Limited Staff Availability for Training and Outreach

Nationally, according to Education's survey of grantee school districts in school year 2010-11, homeless liaisons spent a median amount of nearly 2 hours per week on their responsibilities for the EHCY program.[35] Many liaisons said that they juggled multiple responsibilities, including duties outside of the EHCY program. Officials in 7 of the 20 districts cited their limited availability to provide training and outreach or the lack of sufficiently trained school personnel as a challenge to identifying eligible students. In one state we visited the state EHCY program coordinator who surveyed homeless liaisons on the amount of time they spent on the EHCY program said she has found a link between the amount of time liaisons spend on the EHCY program and the number of homeless students they have identified.

Confusion Regarding Terminology

One liaison said there is confusion around "awaiting foster care placement," a term used to describe some children and youth eligible for the EHCY program. Specifically, the liaison told us that she would receive requests for services for children in foster care, rather than for children awaiting foster care placement.[36] In another district, a liaison said that among the district's many military families, the term "transition," sometimes used to describe eligible families, has a meaning unrelated to homelessness.

Stigma

Officials in 7 of the 20 districts said that stigma around being identified as homeless makes it challenging to identify eligible children and youth. One formerly homeless student we interviewed described her initial

---

[35]The 95 percent confidence interval for this median is from 1.6 to 1.9.

[36]In this state, according to the state educational agency, a child is awaiting foster care placement during the period of time between the initial placement of the child into state care and the 30-day shelter care hearing—at which time the court reviews the status of the child and either orders the child to return home or to remain in placement (i.e. in foster care).

GAO-14-465 Education of Homeless Students

identification as very traumatic because she did not want anyone at school to know about her housing status and did not want to be called homeless. She said she would rather have received bad grades in high school than have her teachers know of her situation. Another said that she did not want anyone to know she was homeless but found it difficult to hide when she had to resort to "couch-surfing" in the homes of many different people.

Identification of Homeless LGBTQ Youth

Some officials we spoke with suggested the districts under-identify unaccompanied homeless youth,[37] including lesbian, gay, bisexual, transgender, or questioning (LGBTQ) youth who tend to be overrepresented in the homeless youth population.[38] Officials in five districts told us they are involved in efforts targeted to LGBTQ youth. For example, an official in one of these districts said the district has been involved in focus groups and worked with service providers on how to better identify and serve these youth who may have separated from their families due to their LGBTQ identification.

Fear of Government

Officials in 5 of 20 districts told us that some families fear being known to government entities, such as child protective services, police, and immigration services. For example, officials in one district said parents may be afraid that the child protective services agency will remove their children from their custody if they are discovered to be homeless.

Natural Disasters

Natural disasters, including floods and a hurricane that forced many families from their homes, also presented challenges for some districts we reviewed. To identify the large numbers of students displaced simultaneously in these districts, officials working in four of five districts we interviewed about their experiences with natural disasters relied heavily on staff and outside resources (e.g., shelters and community meetings).[39] However, officials said that factors such as families'

---

[37]Unaccompanied youth are those not in the physical custody of a parent or guardian. 42 U.S.C. § 11434a(6).

[38]Andrew Cray, Katie Miller, and Laura E. Durso, *Seeking Shelter: The Experiences and Unmet Needs of LGBT Homeless Youth,* Center for American Progress (Washington, D.C.: September 2013).

[39]Officials in one of these districts said they relied on students to self-identify while another district also used previously scheduled parent-teacher conferences to identify students.

unwillingness to self-identify and frequent mobility following the disaster created challenges to identifying and serving students. For example, officials in a district affected by heavy flooding said that immediately following the flooding, families moved in with relatives or other families and did not necessarily consider themselves to be homeless. However, as time passed, the district had to identify families in another wave as families again were displaced from where they initially had moved.

Under-identification can negatively affect homeless students' ability to access needed services and to succeed in school. For example, according to a formerly homeless youth we interviewed, prior to being identified as homeless during his final year of school, he had been receiving Fs on his report card. After being identified, he received a bus pass, school supplies, and a laptop—necessary supplies to help him graduate. Although he faced significant pressures outside of school, according to a school official, and challenges completing his schoolwork, he graduated and was able to obtain employment. Another unaccompanied homeless youth said that after he was identified as homeless he received assistance with school work and clothing for an internship, and was very happy to be able to stay at the same high school. Some officials we interviewed noted that children and youth not connected to school or other services can be particularly challenging to identify, leaving them most at risk of failing to receive necessary services.

Selected School Districts Leveraged Resources to Serve Homeless Students, but Faced Resource and Coordination Challenges

Students experiencing homelessness have diverse needs, ranging from school-related to more basic needs. Nationally, grantee school districts in school year 2010-11 most frequently reported transportation to and from school, family or student preoccupation with survival needs, and frequent mobility from school to school as among homeless students' greatest barriers to school enrollment, attendance, and success, respectively, according to Education's survey of these school districts.[40] Some officials we interviewed cited similar barriers. For example, a high school principal said that the most pressing need for homeless students in his school is for a safe place to sleep, and students who are worried about where they will sleep at night will not be focused on their studies. Some of the homeless youth we spoke with also indicated that stable housing or food

[40]Officials in grantee school districts were asked to select among eight barriers to school enrollment, six barriers to school attendance, and nine barriers to school success, aside from "other (please specify)."

were among their significant needs. Specifically, one unaccompanied homeless youth we interviewed—who has lived with a series of family members since leaving her mother's home—said that while she currently sleeps on the couch in her uncle's house, she worries every day about her next move as she does not know how long she will be allowed to stay.

To help address the needs of homeless students, grantee school districts in school year 2010-11 reported providing a variety of services, according to Education's survey (see fig. 4).

Figure 4: Most Common Services Grantee School Districts Reported Providing to Homeless Children and Youth, School Year 2010-11

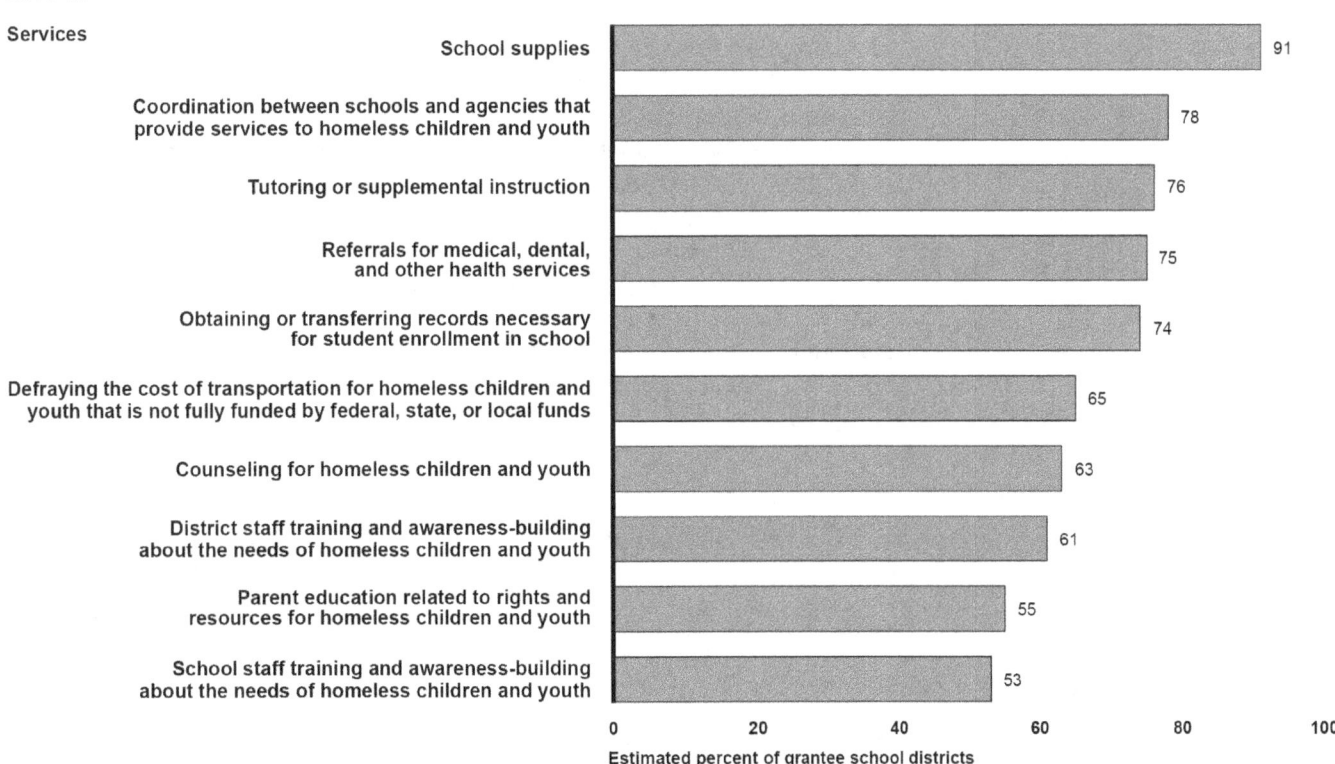

Services

Service	Estimated percent of grantee school districts
School supplies	91
Coordination between schools and agencies that provide services to homeless children and youth	78
Tutoring or supplemental instruction	76
Referrals for medical, dental, and other health services	75
Obtaining or transferring records necessary for student enrollment in school	74
Defraying the cost of transportation for homeless children and youth that is not fully funded by federal, state, or local funds	65
Counseling for homeless children and youth	63
District staff training and awareness-building about the needs of homeless children and youth	61
Parent education related to rights and resources for homeless children and youth	55
School staff training and awareness-building about the needs of homeless children and youth	53

Estimated percent of grantee school districts

Source: GAO analysis of Department of Education survey of grantee school districts. | GAO-14-465

Notes: The figure depicts services that an estimated 50 percent of grantee districts or more reported providing. All estimates in this figure have margins of error of less than six percentage points.

Similarly, the school districts we reviewed provided a range of services and supports to address the various needs of homeless students, which presented some challenges. These include transportation, coordination with other educational services, and partnering with community organizations:

Transportation

Officials we interviewed said their districts provided eligible students with transportation to and from school, as required by the McKinney-Vento Act, through means such as public transit, district buses, taxi cabs, gas assistance and mileage reimbursements.[41] Officials in 9 of the 20 districts also said they collaborated with neighboring districts to transport homeless students across district boundaries, such as by splitting transportation costs or dividing responsibility for routes to and from school.

However, district officials also reported challenges providing transportation due to cost and logistics. Nationally, according to Education's survey of grantee districts in school year 2010-11, an estimated 52 percent of them ranked defraying the cost of transportation among the services on which they spent the most EHCY funds[42] and about one-third of districts (37 percent) reported that coordinating transportation services was among their responsibilities that took the most time. Officials in 7 of the 20 districts we interviewed reported similar challenges. For example, one homeless liaison said that in school year 2011-12 the district spent $550,000 on cabs to transport homeless students.[43] Officials in another district told us of a student who spent 4 hours per day commuting to and from the child's school of origin—the

---

[41]State plans are required to contain assurances that the state and its school districts will adopt policies and practices to ensure that transportation is provided, at the request of the parent or guardian (or in the case of unaccompanied youth, the liaison) to and from the school of origin. 42 U.S.C. § 11432(g)(1)(J)(iii).

[42]The Consolidated Appropriations Act, 2014 authorized school districts to use ESEA Title I funds to provide transportation for homeless students to their schools of origin. Consolidated Appropriations Act, 2014, Pub. L. No. 113-76, div. H, tit. III, 128 Stat. 5, 388 (2013).

[43]Officials told us the district did not receive an EHCY grant. The state's EHCY program coordinator said that to ensure that EHCY grant funds are not used solely to defray the costs of transportation, the state limits the amount of the grant districts can use for transportation purposes to 65 percent.

school that the family had requested.[44] While district officials did not think this was in the best interest of the child, officials said they did not think they could refuse to provide transportation due to the distance.[45] Some district officials we spoke with also said coordinating transportation across districts can be difficult. For example, billing and being billed by other districts can be inefficient and problematic. A district transportation official we interviewed noted the significant amount of administrative work it takes to arrange a student's transportation. For example, she said she could spend an entire day trying to figure out how to free up a bus driver to transport one homeless student to and from school when she also needs to worry about the transportation of another 500 students.

Coordinating Educational Services

Officials in the districts we interviewed coordinated with other education programs and districts to help address homeless students' needs. For example, some districts used ESEA Title I, Part A funds to provide students with tutoring, uniforms, and funds for class fees, as well as hygiene kits, clothing and laundry vouchers, among other things.[46] Officials in 7 of the 20 districts said these funds also supported salaries for positions that support homeless students, such as EHCY program staff, social workers and homeless student advocates. In addition, officials in some districts said they have coordinated with staff from

---

[44]The McKinney-Vento Act requires school districts to place homeless children or youth in either their school of origin or in a public school in the local attendance area where they are actually living, according to the best interest of the child or youth. 42 U.S.C. § 11432(g)(3)(A). In making the best interest determination, the Act states that to the extent feasible, a school district shall keep a student in the school of origin, unless doing so is contrary to the wishes of the parent or guardian. If a district decides to place a student in a school that is not the school of origin or one requested by the parent or guardian, it must provide a written explanation to the parent or guardian along with a statement about their right to appeal the placement decision. 42 U.S.C. § 11432(g)(3)(B).

[45]According to Education guidance, school districts may consider the age of a child or youth, the distance of a commute, and the impact it may have on a student's education, among other things, in determining what is feasible.

[46]According to Education, homeless children and youth are automatically eligible for ESEA Title I, Part A services. Under Title I, Part A, school districts must reserve, or set aside, such funds as are necessary to provide comparable services to homeless children who are not attending Title I schools. 20 U.S.C. § 6313(c)(3)(A). For example, Title I, Part A funds may be used to provide educationally-related support services, such as tutoring, to children at shelters, motels, and other places where homeless children may live. According to officials, Education's regulations also permit school districts to reserve Title I funds to provide support to homeless students who do attend Title I schools. See 34 C.F.R. § 200.77(g).

special education programs to help facilitate services for homeless students; migrant education programs to help identify homeless migrant children; and in some instances, preschool programs to serve homeless preschool-aged children. Officials in 5 of the 20 districts said their preschool programs reserved spaces for homeless preschool-aged children or prioritized these students for services,[47] and in four of these districts, officials said the district transported homeless preschoolers to and from school.[48] Some officials also described coordinating with other districts. For example, officials in three districts said they coordinated with other districts to help homeless students obtain partial credit for work completed elsewhere but said that such efforts could be challenging. In one extraordinary case, we spoke with an official who said he worked for months to obtain a student's transcript from an African refugee camp to be able to eventually verify the student had received 33 credits, exceeding the 22 necessary to graduate. According to a formerly homeless youth we interviewed, receiving credit for work completed was very important to help her meet graduation requirements as she moved across the country twice during high school and attended a total of four high schools.

Officials in 11 of the 20 districts we interviewed cited challenges due to limited staff availability or resources with which to serve homeless students and adequately address their needs. For example, a school principal in a K-8 school we visited without full-time counselors or support staff said homeless students there have access to about 30 percent of the support services the school would like to offer them. In another high school we visited, officials said there is a severe lack of resources at the school to support homeless students. Specifically, according to officials, teachers currently fund a "food closet" on nearly every floor of the high school to meet the needs of hungry students.

---

[47]In some of the districts, the preschool programs officials referred to were Head Start programs. Homeless children who meet the EHCY program definition are automatically eligible for Head Start. Homeless preschoolers are also a target population under the McKinney-Vento Act. For example, each state plan must include procedures to ensure that homeless children have equal access to the same public preschool programs, administered by the state educational agency, as provided to other children in the state. 42 U.S.C. § 11432(g)(1)(F)(i).

[48]In one of these districts, an official said that homeless preschoolers can ride the bus but must be accompanied by a sibling. According to Education guidance, a district must provide transportation for homeless preschoolers only if it provides transportation for other preschoolers.

GAO-14-465 Education of Homeless Students

| Partnering with Community Organizations | To expand their ability to serve homeless students' needs, district and school officials also leveraged community resources to provide students with access to additional services and supports. For example, some officials we interviewed said that they referred homeless students or their families to organizations and agencies that provide health and mental health services, as well as to other community organizations, such as food pantries and shelters for students' pressing needs.[49] Officials in 6 of the 20 districts reported they assisted homeless youth in accessing public benefits, such as for health care or food. Officials in some districts also said they referred students to other federal programs, such as Head Start and Runaway and Homeless Youth (RHY) programs, and housing programs for services.[50] In one district we visited officials said they improved referrals for services by developing trainings for an interagency committee comprised of various community stakeholders on resources and services available to homeless students. However, officials said that a lack of community resources affected their ability to meet student needs. For example, officials in a number of school districts we interviewed (9 of 20) said the lack of available or affordable housing options made it challenging to address the needs of homeless children and their families. |

School districts also played an important role in addressing the needs of students displaced by natural disasters and maintaining their school stability. For example, in the immediate aftermath, officials we interviewed in one of five districts about their experiences with natural disasters said

---

[49]Under the McKinney-Vento Act, liaisons must ensure that homeless children, youth, and their families receive referrals to health care, mental health, dental, and other appropriate services. 42 U.S.C. § 11432(g)(6)(A)(iii).

[50]Officials in four districts said that the use of different federal definitions of homelessness has created some challenges or confusion. Some HUD programs use a definition of homelessness that is different than the EHCY program definition. For example, according to officials we spoke with some families living doubled-up may not be eligible for HUD programs. As we have previously reported, the HEARTH Act of 2009 broadened the definition of homelessness used by HUD homeless assistance programs. However, the HEARTH Act did not fully align the definitions used by the EHCY program and the homeless assistance programs. For example, an individual or family who is sharing housing with others may be eligible for services under the homeless assistance programs, but only if they will imminently lose their housing, have no subsequent residence identified, and lack the resources or support networks need to obtain other permanent housing. Unaccompanied youth and homeless families with children and youth who meet the EHCY program definition may be eligible for homeless assistance programs as well, but only under certain other circumstances. See 42 U.S.C. § 11302(a)(5)-(6).

three schools were used as emergency shelters for families. Officials in four districts said they received a great deal of community support through donations—such as mattresses, heaters, food, clothing and supplies—to help address the significant needs of displaced students and families. However, officials also reported challenges in serving large numbers of newly identified homeless students, sometimes without additional funds for services. For example, one district without EHCY grant funds spent $750,000 to transport displaced students to and from school and to pay tuition to other districts where some students began attending school, according to officials. Maintaining contact with families through their moves was also a challenge for some officials we interviewed. In one district, officials said they were unaware of the number of students who have not returned to their school of origin or who plan to relocate permanently to where they went after the storm. In addition, officials in another district discussed the need for counseling following the trauma that students faced in fleeing and coping with a natural disaster.

Homelessness Following a Natural Disaster

Three families we interviewed who were displaced from their homes following a hurricane—two of whom moved at least twice in the months following—told us of the important role their children's school played in helping to address their many needs. In addition to transportation and school supplies, the school provided homeless families with free before- and after-school care for students, food, gift cards, and clothing—some of which were donated by other organizations, businesses, and school districts, within and outside the state. According to school officials, families were also offered counseling services, though meeting students' needs for counseling has been a challenge. Officials described how children faced significant trauma following the storm. For example, one student carried a sibling on her back to escape rising floodwaters.

Source: Interviews with school officials and families. | GAO-14-465

Federal and State Agencies Use Numerous Strategies to Collaborate to Improve Services to Homeless Students despite Barriers

The Federal EHCY Program Manager Collaborates with Officials from Other Education Programs, Federal Agencies, and States to Increase Awareness about Homeless Education

The federal EHCY program manager collaborates with officials from other Education programs, federal agencies, and states (see table 2).[51] These collaborative efforts are designed to share information with other programs likely to serve homeless students and increase awareness about the EHCY program and the rights of, and services available to, homeless students, among other things. In addition, the EHCY program manager provides training and technical assistance to state program coordinators. GAO has previously found that collaboration is essential for increasing the efficiency and effectiveness of federal programs and activities in areas where multiple agencies or programs have similar goals, engage in similar activities, or target similar beneficiaries.[52]

Table 2: Selected Examples of Federal Education for Homeless Children and Youth (EHCY) Program Collaboration Activities within the Department of Education, with Other Federal Agencies, and with States

Examples of collaboration activities with officials and staff from other Department of Education (Education) programs, offices, or initiatives	Collaboration partners within Education[a]
• EHCY program manager presents information to individuals responsible for implementing other Education programs, according to the EHCY program manager.	*Officials responsible for administering:* • Elementary and Secondary Education Act, Title I, Part A programs • Migrant Education Program • Elementary and Secondary Education Act, Title III programs[b]
• Officials from other Education programs/offices present at EHCY state coordinator conferences, according to the EHCY program manager.	*Officials responsible for administering:* • Migrant Education Program • Office of Special Education and Rehabilitative Services programs • Early Learning Initiative (Office of Early Learning)
• Officials from other Education programs/offices present at the annual National Association for the Education of Homeless Children and Youth conference, according to the EHCY program manager.	*Officials responsible for administering:* • Elementary and Secondary Education Act, Title I, Part A programs • Office of Safe and Healthy Students programs

[51]The federal EHCY program manager has primary responsibility for overseeing the EHCY grant making process; providing technical assistance, including serving as the contract representative for NCHE; program monitoring and oversight; reviewing program performance data; and coordinating interagency collaboration efforts.

[52]GAO-13-279SP.

Examples of collaboration activities with officials and staff from other Department of Education (Education) programs, offices, or initiatives	Collaboration partners within Education[a]
• Officials from other Education programs generally review materials developed by the National Center for Homeless Education (NCHE) that pertain to their programs, according to Education officials.	*Officials responsible for administering:* • Elementary and Secondary Education Act, Title I, Part A programs • Migrant Education Program • Office of Special Education and Rehabilitative Services programs • Office of Early Learning programs
• EHCY program manager discusses relevant issues with staff from other Education programs, such as data on the number of students applying for financial aid for college as "independent," according to the EHCY program manager.[c]	• Office of Postsecondary Education

Examples of collaboration activities with other federal agencies and entities	**Collaboration partners from other federal agencies/entities**
• As a member of the U.S. Interagency Council on Homelessness (USICH), Education shares responsibility with other agencies in fulfilling the council's mission to "coordinate the Federal response to homelessness and to create a national partnership at every level of government and with the private sector to reduce and end homelessness in the nation while maximizing the effectiveness of the Federal Government in contributing to the end of homelessness."[d]	• U.S. Interagency Council on Homelessness
• Initiative to facilitate data sharing at the local level, according to Education and other federal officials.[e]	• U.S. Interagency Council on Homelessness • Department of Housing and Urban Development
• Initiative to better understand how to prevent homelessness among lesbian, gay, bisexual, transgender, or questioning (LGBTQ) youth.	• U.S. Interagency Council on Homelessness • Department of Housing and Urban Development • Department of Health and Human Services • Department of Justice

Examples of collaboration activities with states	

• Provides technical assistance and training to state EHCY program coordinators, as required by the McKinney-Vento Act, often through NCHE.[f]
   o NCHE develops and shares issue briefs, tool kits, and other materials; disseminates information via its website and listserv; conducts training webinars and self-paced online training; and operates a helpline available to state and local EHCY program officials and staff, and others.
• Provided additional technical assistance after recent natural disasters, according to Education and state officials.
   o NCHE is hosting a natural disaster workgroup of state EHCY program coordinators to develop a new section of the state coordinator handbook on preparing for, and responding to, natural disasters, according to Education and state officials.	

Source: GAO analysis of documentation and interviews with officials from the Department of Education, other federal agencies, and states. | GAO-14-465

[a]Selected examples of Education offices, programs, and initiatives with which the EHCY program manager collaborates.

[b]Title III of the Elementary and Secondary Education Act of 1965 (ESEA), as amended, authorizes federal funding for language instruction for limited English proficient and immigrant students.

[c]A student's dependency status determines whose financial information he or she is required to provide when filling out the Free Application for Federal Student Aid to apply for federal financial aid for college or university. Students determined to be "dependent" must provide financial information about their parents as well as themselves, whereas students determined to be "independent" must only provide their own financial information (and their spouse's if married). By law, unaccompanied homeless youth are considered "independent" and do not have to provide their parents' financial information. 20 U.S.C. § 1087vv(d)(1)(H).

[d]42 U.S.C. § 11311. USICH has developed a federal strategic plan to prevent and end homelessness called Opening Doors: Federal Strategic Plan to Prevent and End Homelessness. This plan has four main goals. They are (1) Finishing the job of ending chronic homelessness by 2015; (2) Preventing and ending homelessness among veterans by 2015; (3) Preventing and ending homelessness for families, youth, and children by 2020; and (4) Setting a path to ending all types of homelessness. USICH monitors and reports on the progress of implementation of the strategic plan, including the activities of agencies and programs.

[e]HUD officials told us that they have also collaborated with the EHCY program manager, HHS, and USICH on initiatives to obtain an accurate count of children and youth experiencing homelessness and better understand the characteristics of those children and youth, and with the EHCY program manager and USICH on aligning housing status indicators and developing a cross walk of definitions of homelessness across programs to improve local collaboration and data analysis. In addition HUD has worked with the EHCY program manager on an initiative to identify and spread innovative practices employed by homeless housing providers to ensure fair and equal education of homeless children and youth, according to HUD officials.

[f]Education is required to provide support and technical assistance to a state educational agency to assist it in carrying out its EHCY responsibilities, if requested by the state educational agency. 42 U.S.C. § 11434(b).

State Educational Agencies Collaborate with Other State Agencies, Service Providers, and School Districts

State EHCY program coordinators collaborate with other state agencies, service providers and school districts to improve services to homeless children and youth. The McKinney-Vento Act requires state EHCY coordinators to facilitate coordination between the state educational agency and other state agencies and to collaborate with school district homeless liaisons, service providers, and community organizations, among others.[53] According to Education data from its survey of state EHCY program coordinators covering school year 2010-11, 30 state coordinators ranked coordinating with other organizations and agencies to provide and improve services to homeless children and youth among the three activities on which they spend the most time.[54] Thirty-six state coordinators reported that building programmatic linkages among various programs, agencies, or organizations was among the top three

[53]42 U.S.C. § 11432(f)(4)(5).

[54]Providing technical assistance was the only activity that more state coordinators (42) reported among the top three activities on which they spend their time. In addition, 24 ranked raising awareness and understanding among districts of the requirements of the McKinney-Vento Act and the role of the district homeless liaison among the top three activities.

collaboration efforts that improved program administration and/or services to homeless children and youth (see fig. 5).

Figure 5: Time Spent on Collaboration and Top Collaboration Activities, Reported by State Education for Homeless Children and Youth (EHCY) Program Coordinators for School Year 2010-11

Number of state EHCY program coordinators who ranked coordination among the top three activities on which they spend time

30 out of 50 | 30 |

Number of state EHCY program coordinators who ranked various coordination and collaboration activities among top three for improving EHCY program or services

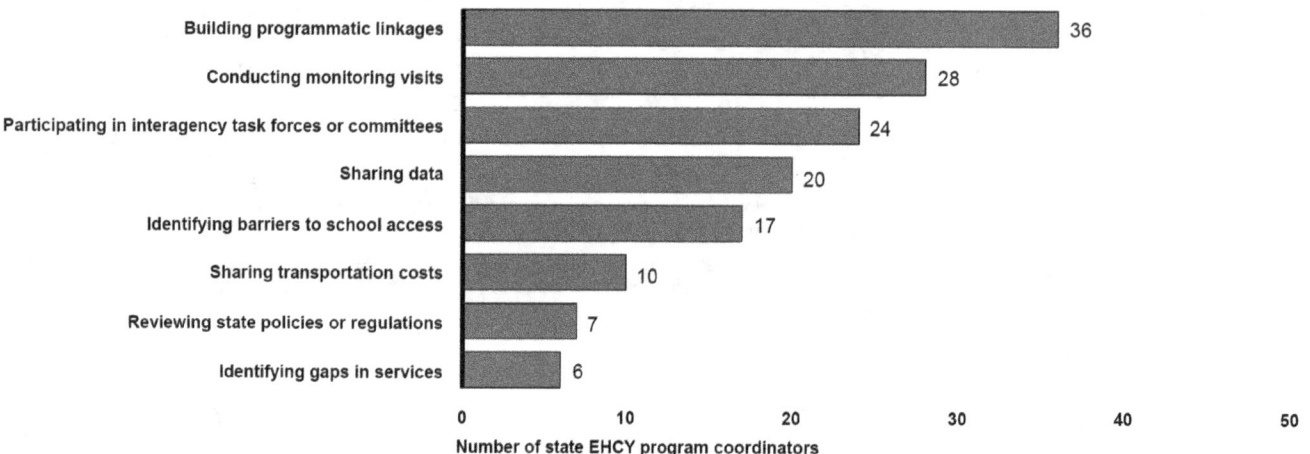

Source: GAO analysis of Department of Education survey of states. | GAO-14-465

The collaborative activities state EHCY program coordinators engage in may vary depending on whether they are collaborating with school districts, other programs, interagency councils, or non-governmental entities (see fig. 6).

Figure 6: Examples of State Education for Homeless Children and Youth Program Collaboration Activities

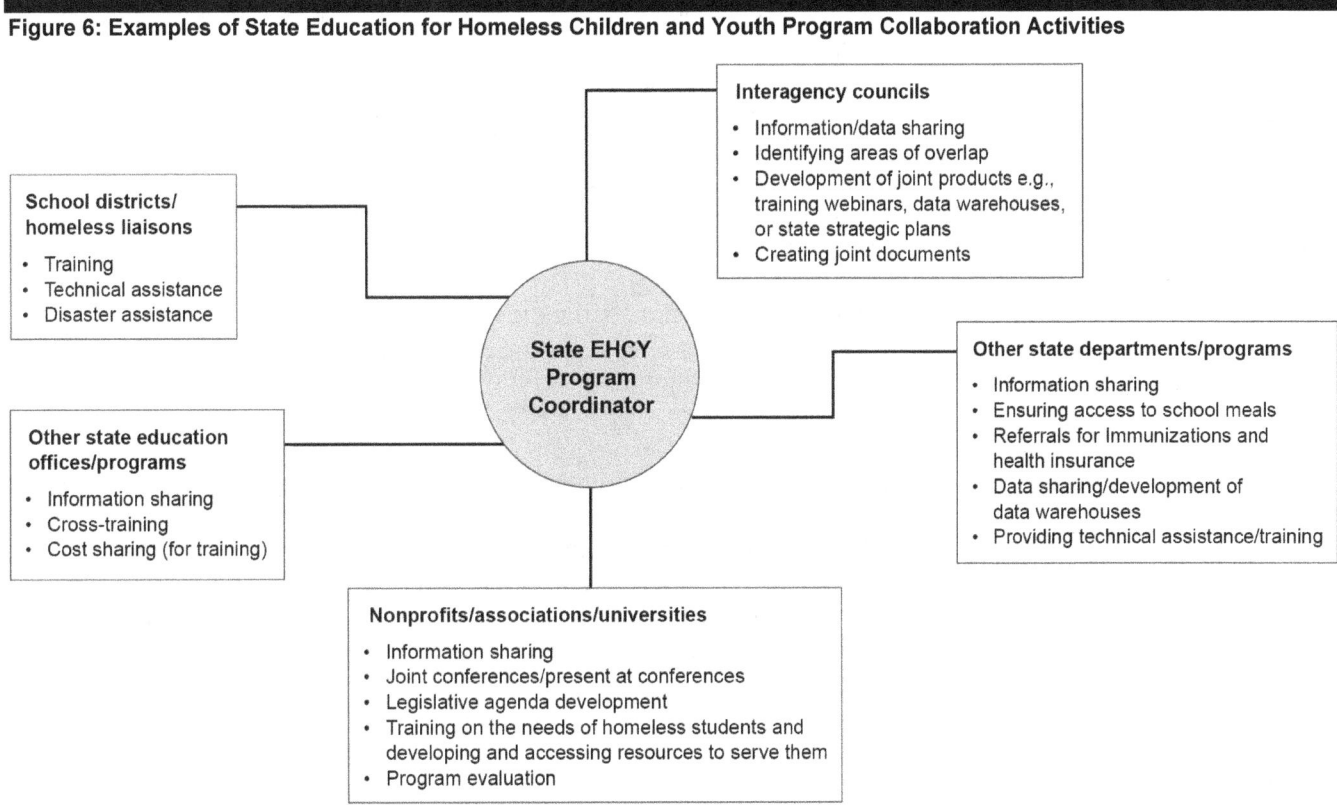

Source: GAO analysis of interviews with state EHCY program coordinators. | GAO-14-465

State EHCY program collaboration activities with other state agencies, programs, service providers, and associations have included raising awareness of the program, developing joint products, such as strategic plans, and efforts to better connect students to services. For example, state EHCY program staff in one state told us they collaborate with the state's health department and Children's Health Insurance Program to make sure students have access to immunizations and help homeless families apply for health insurance for their children. Additionally, they collaborate with the state agriculture department to ensure homeless children have immediate access to free school meals. One state coordinator told us that she has partnered with the 21st Century Community Learning Centers (21st CCLC) program, which allowed the state to increase the number of high schools receiving 21st CCLC funding

GAO-14-465 Education of Homeless Students

from 5 to 37 and increased the resources available to serve homeless students.[55] In addition, three state coordinators we spoke with told us that they have worked with universities in their states to, for example, provide information about students experiencing homelessness and barriers they face to higher education. Officials in one state told us that this collaboration has led over 30 public institutions of higher learning to identify a single point of contact within the school to advocate for homeless students.

State EHCY program coordinators we interviewed provide technical assistance and training to school districts, as required by the McKinney-Vento Act,[56] but the amount and type of assistance varies, particularly in districts that do not receive EHCY grants. According to Education's survey of state EHCY program coordinators, nearly half (24 of 50), responded that providing technical assistance was the activity on which they spend the most time, and 42 said it was among the top three activities. While district homeless liaisons we spoke with generally told us that they receive a good deal of technical assistance and support from their state coordinator, in one state we visited, non-grantee school district liaisons told us that they have limited interactions with their state coordinator.

Federal and State Agencies Face Similar Barriers to Greater Collaboration

Both federal and state officials frequently cited limited staff capacity as a barrier to greater collaboration. At the federal level, the EHCY program is administered by Education's Office of Student Achievement and School Accountability (SASA) and run largely by a single individual – the EHCY program manager. The EHCY program manager has primary responsibility for administering the EHCY program. In addition, this individual is responsible for overseeing a second Education program – ESEA Title I, Part D (Prevention and Intervention Programs for Children and Youth Who Are Neglected, Delinquent, or At Risk). The EHCY program manager told us that capacity is a challenge to additional

---

[55]The 21st Century Community Learning Centers (21st CCLC) program is an Education program which supports the creation of community learning centers that provide academic enrichment opportunities during non-school hours for children, particularly students who attend high-poverty and low-performing schools. Some states, if they are approved for a waiver by Education, may also offer expanded learning time programs within the school day.

[56]42 U.S.C. § 11432(f)(6).

collaboration. For example, he only attends conferences for Title I and other Education programs every few years. Similarly, while state EHCY program coordinators we spoke with generally felt that there is significant collaboration with other entities, several also told us that staff capacity was a significant barrier to further collaboration. State coordinators are generally responsible for managing the EHCY grant process, monitoring and overseeing implementation of the EHCY program at the school district level, and providing technical assistance and training to school district personnel, including homeless liaisons; sometimes in several hundred school districts. Many state coordinators have responsibilities in addition to those for the EHCY program. According to Education's survey data from school year 2010-11, 23 of the 50 state EHCY program coordinators reported working 30 hours or more per week on EHCY program responsibilities. The same survey found that more than half of the states (27) had one or fewer full-time employees working in the state EHCY program office (see fig. 7). For example, one state coordinator we spoke with was also the coordinator for another education program, which she said takes up about 40 percent of her time.[57]

---

[57]While such arrangements might facilitate collaboration between the two programs under the same coordinator, it may also create challenges to collaboration with other programs due to the additional responsibilities of that single individual for multiple programs.

Figure 7: Hours Worked by State Education for Homeless Children and Youth (EHCY) Program Coordinators and Number of Paid Staff in State EHCY Program Offices for School Year 2010-11

Number of hours worked per week by 50 state EHCY program coordinators in their official capacity as state coordinator

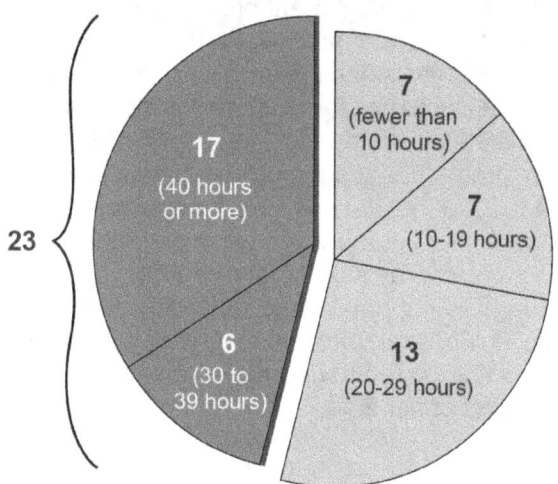

Number of paid staff, including state EHCY program coordinator, in 50 state EHCY program offices

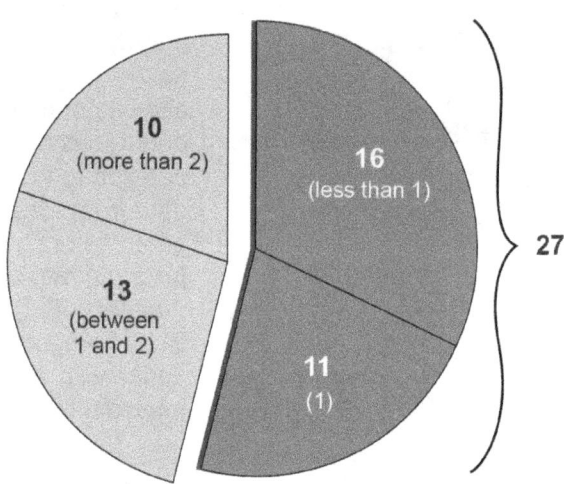

Source: GAO analysis of Department of Education survey of states. | GAO-14-465

According to state EHCY program coordinators, resource constraints have prevented additional collaboration efforts. For example, three state coordinators told us they must choose which partners to collaborate with at the expense of others. In one of these states, this has meant limited collaboration with RHY programs. In GAO's previous work, we have emphasized the importance of agencies identifying and leveraging sufficient funding to accomplish their objectives and to initiate or sustain their collaborative efforts and we suggested approaches to help them do so.[58]

Federal and state officials also said that differing definitions of who is considered "homeless" under various federal programs was another

---

[58]GAO, *Managing for Results: Key Considerations for Implementing Interagency Collaborative Mechanisms*, GAO-12-1022 (Washington, D.C.: Sept. 27, 2012); GAO, *Results-Oriented Government: Practices that Can Help Enhance and Sustain Collaboration among Federal Agencies*, GAO-06-15 (Washington, D.C.: Oct. 21, 2005); GAO, *Managing for Results: Implementation Approaches Used to Enhance Collaboration in Interagency Groups*, GAO-14-220 (Washington, D.C.: Feb. 14, 2014).

barrier to collaboration.[59] Because the population eligible for services under each program differs, the populations contained in data collected by one agency will be different than in data collected by other agencies, making data sharing more difficult. The federal EHCY program manager told us that the lack of a consistent definition across programs administered by Education and HUD has created a challenge to increasing data sharing at the local level between school districts and Continuums of Care (CoC).[60] Because a relatively small number of students considered homeless under Education's definition may be eligible for services funded by CoCs, these entities sometimes feel that the additional work necessary to share the data is not worthwhile, according to the EHCY program manager. Nationally, most homeless students are "doubled up." Officials from one state told us that because this is the case in their state, though school districts want to provide wrap-around services that meet the wide variety of homeless youths' needs,

---

[59]GAO has previously reported on the lack of a common definition of homelessness across federal agencies and programs. See GAO, *Homelessness: A Common Vocabulary Could Help Agencies Collaborate and Collect More Consistent Data*, GAO-10-702 (Washington, D.C.: June 30, 2010). As we reported in 2012, the HEARTH Act of 2009 broadened the definition of homelessness used by HUD homeless assistance programs. See GAO, *Homelessness: Fragmentation and Overlap in Programs Highlight the Need to Identify, Assess, and Reduce Inefficiencies*, GAO-12-491 (Washington, D.C.: May 10, 2012). However, the HEARTH Act did not fully align the definitions used by the EHCY program and the homeless assistance programs.

[60]The CoC program is designed to assist individuals (including unaccompanied youth) and families experiencing homelessness and to provide the services needed to help such individuals move into transitional and permanent housing, with the goal of long-term stability. The program is designed to promote community-wide planning and strategic use of resources to address homelessness; improve coordination and integration with mainstream resources and other programs targeted to people experiencing homelessness; improve data collection and performance measurement; and allow each community to tailor its program to the particular strengths and challenges within that community. HUD awards CoC program funding competitively to nonprofit organizations, states, and/or units of general purpose local governments, which may contract or subgrant with other organizations or government entities to carry out the grant's day-to-day program operations.

these students may be ineligible for services through HUD programs.[61] However, one school district in one of the states we reviewed has entered into an agreement with the local CoC that allows school district personnel to access and enter data into the CoC's Homeless Management Information System. This partnership allows the school district and CoC partners to track the services homeless students have received, evaluate the need for additional services, and make referrals for those services, among other functions. A state EHCY program coordinator we spoke with told us that a common definition would allow Education and HUD programs to pool data, increasing collaboration and efficiency. This official said that instead of redundant data collection, resources could be used to provide additional services.

Education Currently Lacks a Comprehensive Oversight Plan and Faces Limitations in Using its Performance Data to Assess Program Results

---

[61]Under the EHCY program, homeless children and youth include those who are sharing the housing of others due to loss of housing, economic hardship, or a similar reason. 42 U.S.C. § 11434a(2)(B)(i). Under the Continuum of Care program, an individual or family who is sharing housing with others may be considered homeless, but only if they will imminently lose their housing, have no subsequent residence identified, and lack the resources or support networks need to obtain other permanent housing. Unaccompanied youth and homeless families with children and youth who meet the EHCY program definition may meet the definition of homeless for the Continuum of Care program as well, but only under certain other circumstances. See 42 U.S.C. § 11302(a)(5)-(6).

Education Has Protocols for Monitoring State EHCY Programs but Lacks a Plan to Ensure Oversight of All States

Education has protocols and procedures in place to monitor state EHCY programs. According to Education guidance, monitoring is the regular and systematic examination of a state's administration and implementation of a federal education grant, contract, or cooperative agreement.[62] To hold states accountable to provide a free appropriate public education to homeless students,[63] Education evaluates the degree to which states meet certain standards, called monitoring indicators[64] (see appendix II). These include data on:

- monitoring of school districts;
- implementation of procedures to identify, enroll, and retain homeless students by coordinating and collaborating with other program offices and state agencies;
- provision of technical assistance to school districts;
- efforts to ensure that school district grant plans for services to eligible homeless students meet all requirements;
- compliance with statutory and other regulatory requirements governing the reservation of funds for state-level coordination activities; and
- prompt resolution of disputes.

Education's monitoring involves a review of documents, followed by an on-site or videoconference review, and preparation of a final report that includes any compliance findings for which the state must take corrective

---

[62]In addition, GAO's *Standards for Internal Control in the Federal Government* state that internal control should generally be designed to assure that ongoing monitoring occurs in the course of normal operations, is performed continually, and is ingrained in the agency's operations. See GAO, *Standards for Internal Control in the Federal Government*, GAO/AIMD-00-21.3.1 (Washington, D.C.: November 1999).

[63]The McKinney-Vento Act requires Education to determine the extent to which state educational agencies are ensuring that each homeless child and youth has access to a free appropriate public education. 42 U.S.C. § 11434. In some states, preschool programs are operated under the authority of entities other than the state educational agency or school districts. Because the McKinney-Vento Act requirements only apply to state educational agencies and school districts, Education has no role in monitoring homeless education in preschool programs operated by other entities.

[64]U.S. Department of Education, *Student Achievement and School Accountability Programs (SASA) Monitoring Plan for Formula Grant Programs* (March 2013). The published indicators provide guidance for all states regarding the purpose and intended outcomes of monitoring by describing what is being monitored and providing the criteria for judging the quality of implementation.

action (see fig. 8).[65] Between fiscal years 2007 and 2009, Education's policy was to monitor 50 states and 3 other areas (i.e., 53 "states")[66] at least once during that 3-year time period and it followed this policy.

Figure 8: Overview of Education's Monitoring Process for the Education for Homeless Children and Youth Program

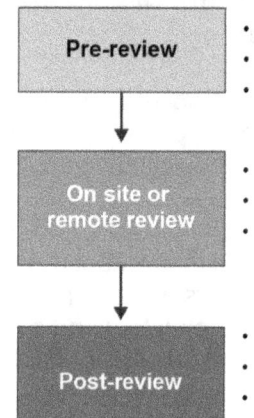

Pre-review
- Select which states to monitor each year
- Contact state educational agency to request documents in advance
- Review documents

On site or remote review
- Interview two or three school districts, including one non-grantee district
- Interview state educational agency officials
- Conduct exit meeting with state educational agency officials to discuss findings

Post-review
- Prepare monitoring report
- Send monitoring report to state
- Follow up with state to ensure that findings are resolved
- Take corrective action if state does not resolve findings in timely way

Source: GAO analysis of Department of Education documents and interviews. | GAO-14-465

Starting in fiscal year 2010, Education adopted a risk-based approach to select states for monitoring to more efficiently target and prioritize limited resources, resulting in longer gaps between monitoring visits in some states. Education conducts an annual risk assessment to evaluate which states have the highest risk of noncompliance, according to the EHCY program manager. The agency weighs the following four risk assessment criteria equally: the state's academic proficiency levels for students experiencing homelessness, the tenure of the state EHCY program coordinator, whether there are multiple or recurring EHCY monitoring

---

[65]A finding is a compliance issue that has a required corrective action by the state educational agency.

[66]In addition to the 50 states, Education's Office of Student Achievement and School Accountability (SASA) also monitors the District of Columbia, the Commonwealth of Puerto Rico, and the Bureau of Indian Education. For the purposes of this report, we refer to all of these as states. Education also provides EHCY grants to the outlying areas (the U.S. Virgin Islands, Guam, American Samoa, and the Northern Mariana Islands), but according to SASA officials these areas consolidate their eligible federal funds under Title V and are therefore monitored by a different office, the Office of School Support and Rural Programs, within the Office of Elementary and Secondary Education.

findings, and a financial review of the state's EHCY grant expenditures.[67] Education also considers the size of the state's EHCY grant allocation and the length of time since a state was last monitored. Since Education adopted this approach in fiscal year 2010, it has monitored 31 of the 53 states for the EHCY program—28 from October 2009 to September 2012 and 3 from October 2012 to July 2014. Of the 22 remaining states, Education last monitored 7 states in fiscal year 2007, 6 in fiscal year 2008, and 9 in fiscal year 2009 (see fig. 9).

Figure 9: Frequency of Federal Monitoring for Education for Homeless Children and Youth (EHCY) Program Compliance since Fiscal Year 2007

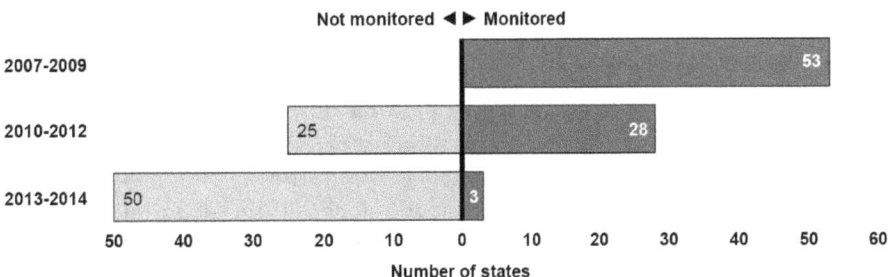

Source: GAO analysis of Department of Education documents. | GAO-14-465

Note: Between fiscal years 2007 and 2009, Education monitored 53 entities for EHCY compliance, including the 50 states, the District of Columbia, the Commonwealth of Puerto Rico, and the Bureau of Indian Education. For the purposes of this report, we refer to all of these as states.

In the fall of 2012 Education began monitoring states that had received waivers from certain ESEA requirements under an initiative Education calls "ESEA Flexibility" and since that time, has monitored three states for

---

[67]Education's final determination of the level of risk averages the risk levels for its EHCY program as well as for another Education program under Title I, Part D (State Agency Program for Neglected and Delinquent Children and Youth), which uses the same criteria.

compliance with the EHCY program.[68] Under Education's ESEA flexibility initiative, 44 of the 53 states[69] currently have waivers from specific requirements of the ESEA, as amended. In these states, Education has conducted regular monitoring, but the monitoring only covers compliance with the ESEA waiver requirements and does not include monitoring for compliance with the EHCY program. As a result, the states with ESEA waivers currently have little EHCY program oversight at the federal level.[70] Education officials cited the shift to a risk-based approach to monitoring the EHCY program, the more recent need to focus on ESEA flexibility waiver monitoring, and a lack of staff capacity as the primary reasons why they have not been able to monitor the states as frequently in recent years as in the past. Education officials said they intend to continue to monitor the EHCY program in the future, but the agency has not determined when or how it will do so. Standards for internal control emphasize the need for federal agencies to establish plans to help ensure goals and objectives can be met, including compliance with applicable laws and regulations.[71] Absent a plan for future monitoring of grantees, Education cannot be sure that problems will be identified and resolved promptly.

As a result of reducing the number of monitoring visits, Education has been unaware of the compliance status of some states for an extended

---

[68]The ESEA authorizes the Secretary of Education to waive, with certain exceptions, any statutory or regulatory requirement of ESEA for states or school districts that receive ESEA funds and submit a waiver request that meets statutory requirements. 20 U.S.C. § 7861. In 2011, Education invited states to request waivers of specific requirements of the ESEA, as amended. To be approved, Education required states to develop and implement specified changes, including comprehensive plans to improve educational outcomes for all students, close achievement gaps, increase equity, and improve the quality of instruction. Education reviewed requests and granted waivers to 45 states through school year 2013–14; however, one state's waiver is not being renewed after the 2013-14 school year, making the current total 44 states with waivers. Under the ESEA, waivers can be effective for up to 4 years, although they may be extended. These waivers do not exempt states from requirements of the McKinney-Vento Act.

[69]The states currently without ESEA waivers are the Bureau of Indian Education, California, Iowa, Montana, Nebraska, North Dakota, Vermont, Washington, and Wyoming.

[70]According to Education officials, although the agency has not conducted on-site monitoring of the EHCY program for these states, it has conducted annual risk assessments and analyzed state and school district performance data. Officials also said that Education responds to complaints it may receive and provides technical assistance.

[71]See GAO/AIMD-00-21.3.1.

period of time. According to GAO's Standards for Internal Control in the Federal Government, monitoring is a key management tool that helps agencies assess the quality of performance over time and ensure that the problems are promptly resolved.[72] Additionally, one state EHCY program coordinator we interviewed said that federal monitoring ensures a higher level of compliance with the McKinney-Vento Act and that it is in a state's best interest to be monitored regularly. According to this program coordinator, monitoring helps states improve how they address homeless students' needs and provides important leverage within the state to ensure that program funds are used as intended. Of the 22 states that Education has not monitored since at least fiscal year 2009, 10 had been required to take corrective actions following their last review to address compliance concerns. While Education found these actions to be sufficient, according to officials, Education is currently unaware of whether these states have remained in compliance and it is possible that they (or other states) may have new or recurring compliance issues. For example, one of the states we visited had not monitored its grantees on-site since school year 2008-09, whereas NCHE recommends states monitor grantees on-site at least once every 3 years.

Because of Education's limited monitoring of some states, it may not be aware of states' current practices and whether they comply with program requirements and their state plans, which Education has not required states to update since 2002.[73] According to agency officials, Education has not requested updates to state plans because it has been waiting for the next reauthorization of the EHCY program before requesting new state plans.[74] The EHCY program manager said that the agency reviews state plans as part of its monitoring review and that some states have

---

[72]See GAO/AIMD-00-21.3.1.

[73]Under the McKinney-Vento Act, states are required to develop plans that describe how they will implement the program and submit the plans to Education. 42 U.S.C. § 11432(g). Education is responsible for reviewing state plans using a peer review process and evaluating whether state laws, policies, and practices described in the plan adequately address the problems of homeless children and youths relating to access to education and placement as described in the plan. 42 U.S.C. § 11434(a).

[74]The EHCY program was last reauthorized as part of the ESEA reauthorization in 2002. Reauthorization of the EHCY program is again being considered as part of future ESEA reauthorization, according to Education officials. Education officials said that clearance from the Office of Management and Budget would be needed before they can require states to update their state plans.

GAO-14-465 Education of Homeless Students

updated their plans with new activities and goals.[75] Some states have implemented programmatic changes since the plans were initially required in 2002. For example, one state we visited changed its service delivery model in recent years by adopting a regional approach to award grants to lead school districts that are responsible for providing services to other districts in their region. This state's EHCY coordinator confirmed that the state has not submitted any state plan updates to Education since 2002. However, because Education is no longer consistently monitoring all states for compliance, the agency is also unable to determine whether states' current practices are consistent with their existing state plan. GAO's Standards for Internal Control in the Federal Government suggest that management continually assess and evaluate whether internal control activities—such as reviewing and monitoring compliance with state plans—are effective and up-to-date.[76]

Education Survey Data and GAO's Review Showed that States Generally Focused Their Monitoring on Grantee Districts and Not Non-Grantee Districts

The McKinney-Vento Act requires each state to describe in its plan how it will ensure that all school districts comply with EHCY program requirements, but does not specify how states must monitor compliance or where they should focus their efforts.[77] NCHE's guidance[78] to states on monitoring districts acknowledges the challenge of monitoring all districts on site annually—given resource constraints—and recommends that states utilize a combination of strategies, such as on-site monitoring for grantee districts and desk monitoring, i.e., phone calls or written correspondence, for non-grantee districts. According to Education's survey of states in school year 2010-11, states use a variety of approaches in monitoring districts. Most states (43 out of 50) monitored grantees on-site and about half (26 out of 50) did so for non-grantees. States also commonly use desk monitoring, with about two-thirds (34 out of 50) using this approach for grantees and about half (26 out of 50) doing so for non-grantees (see table 3).

---

[75]Education is currently developing a template that will allow states to voluntarily update their state plans online, according to officials; however, they said this website is unlikely to be completed before next year.

[76]See GAO/AIMD-00-21.3.1.

[77]42 U.S.C. § 11432(g)(2)(A).

[78]NCHE has developed various resources which are available to assist state EHCY program coordinators ensure their monitoring efforts are effective, for example a state coordinator's handbook for monitoring.

Table 3: Number of States Using Various Approaches to Monitor Districts, School Year 2010-11

Monitoring approaches	Grantee districts	Non-grantee districts
Efforts are monitored through visits to local school districts	43	26
Assurances of compliance with regulations are required	41	25
Efforts are monitored through phone calls or written correspondence (i.e., desk monitoring)	34	26
Efforts are monitored by integrated monitoring visits to school districts that address this and other federal or state programs	33	29
Progress reports are required	23	5
Progress reports are requested	13	6
Efforts are not monitored	0	2

Source: GAO analysis of Education's survey of states. | GAO-14-465

Note: These results are based on a survey of 50 states.

The majority of states in Education's survey also reported including the EHCY program in the state's monitoring of other federal programs for both grantee districts (33 out of 50) and non-grantee districts (29 out of 50).[79] States that monitor compliance for the EHCY program in this way are able to reach additional districts without adding to the state EHCY program coordinator's responsibilities, one of a few strategies that NCHE recommends to cover a large number of districts. For example, in one state we visited, a review team monitors about 100 school districts per year with a lengthy checklist for federal programs that includes the EHCY program.

States focused their monitoring on districts that had received an EHCY grant from the state, resulting in limited oversight of many non-grantee districts. NCHE's guidance indicates that states should monitor grantees at least once during the grant cycle—which can be up to 3 years—and non-grantees at least once every 3-to-5 years.[80] According to Education's

---

[79]However, the survey data do not show whether this monitoring addresses all aspects of the EHCY program or if it just asks about financial elements related to the EHCY program, which is the case for two of the four states we reviewed.

[80]U.S. Department of Education, National Center for Homeless Education, *State Coordinator's Handbook for LEA Monitoring* (Fall 2006), *State Coordinators' Handbook* (December 2010*)*, and *A Guide to Meeting Compliance Requirements for the McKinney-Vento Program* (December 2011).

survey, most states (39 out of the 46 that responded to this question) said that they monitor grantees at least once every 2 years. Half (23 out of 46) of the states that responded to this question reported monitoring non-grantees at least once every 2 years and the other half reported monitoring them less frequently (see fig. 10). Additionally, 2 of 50 states reported that they did not monitor non-grantees at all (see table 3).

Figure 10: Frequency of State Monitoring of Grantee and Non-grantee Districts, by Number of States, School Year 2010-11

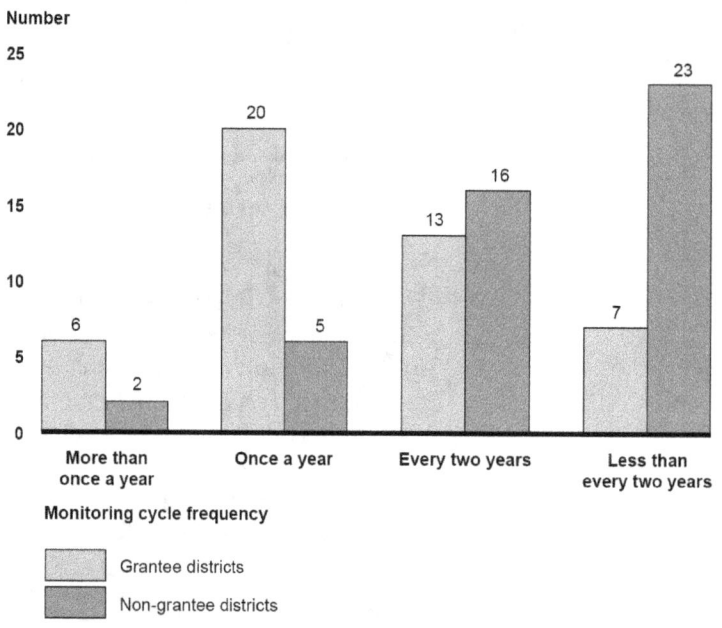

Source: GAO analysis of Department of Education survey of states. | GAO-14-465

Note: 46 out of the 50 states surveyed responded to this survey question.

Similarly, state EHCY program coordinators in three of the four states we reviewed focused on monitoring grantees and employed a variety of approaches, according to our interviews with the coordinators. One state coordinator reported monitoring all grantee school districts on-site annually. Two state coordinators reported monitoring grantees annually using a combination of on-site visits and desk reviews, in which grantees are monitored via phone and email and must send data to the state for review. The fourth state coordinator we interviewed reported conducting quarterly fiscal and program reviews in lieu of formal on-site or desk monitoring for all of the grantees since school year 2008-09.[81]

The four states we reviewed also varied with regard to how often they monitor non-grantees. State coordinators in two of the four states we reviewed regularly monitor all non-grantee districts within the 3 to 5 year timeframe NCHE suggests. One state coordinator reported monitoring non-grantees on a 3-year rotational basis. Another state coordinator uses desk monitoring for all non-grantees annually and also uses a risk-based approach to select non-grantees for on-site monitoring.[82] The other two state coordinators we interviewed do not regularly monitor non-grantees within the suggested timeframe; however, one of these states annually ensures that all districts have identified a homeless liaison.

States may not focus monitoring efforts on non-grantee districts because they lack tools to enforce compliance. One state coordinator explained that the state can record a finding of noncompliance, but because there is no direct fiscal action or penalty attached to it, the district may disregard it. Another state coordinator said she has to accept a district's report of zero homeless students, even if she suspects that the district may be under-identifying them. In contrast, state coordinators we spoke with said that states can hold districts with EHCY grant funding more accountable because they have more direct leverage over them, in the form of the grant. According to Education's survey of states, 3 of 39 states that responded to this question reported that they withheld funds from grantees that were out of compliance.

Monitoring is a key management tool for states to ensure districts' compliance with the McKinney-Vento Act and statewide accountability for administration of the federal grant. In the state that had not monitored its grantee districts on-site since school year 2008-09, we found that not all

---

[81]According to the state coordinator in the state that had not monitored grantee districts on-site since school year 2008-09, the state educational agency will start to monitor grantee districts on-site at least once every 2 years, starting in April 2014.

[82]This state's EHCY program coordinator reported annually reviewing each district's data on homeless students and visiting those non-grantees with the highest risk of noncompliance based on several risk factors, such as fewer than expected homeless students identified given a district's poverty rates; trends in under-identification; a high number of disputes with neighboring districts and/or complaints from parents; and the size of the district, with larger districts assumed to have a higher risk of noncompliance.

districts were aware of the availability of services through the regional structure adopted by the state. This state uses a regional approach for its grantee districts, whereby the grants are distributed to lead entities that are in turn responsible for ensuring that all homeless students within the region receive appropriate services. To do this, the grantee district may provide funds and/or services, such as training, to other districts in its region. While we met with two lead grantee school districts that provided services to other districts in the region, we also met with two other non-grantee districts whose officials were unaware that the district was eligible for funds or services from their respective lead grantee districts, indicating that the state's regional model was not being implemented effectively. Such problems suggest inadequate state-level monitoring of school districts, reinforcing the importance of effective federal monitoring of states.

Education Collects Performance Data but Faces Limitations in Using Them to Assess Program Results

Education relies on annual state performance data collected from school districts to determine the extent to which states are meeting the program's intended goal of ensuring that homeless students have access to a free appropriate public education (see table 4).[83]

Table 4: Required Data Elements from Grantee and Non-grantee School Districts

	Grantee districts	Non-grantee districts
Number of homeless students enrolled[a]	√	√
Number of homeless students served[b]	√	
Subgroups of homeless students enrolled (unaccompanied youth, migratory children and youth, children with disabilities, and Limited English Proficient students)	√	√
Subgroups of homeless students served	√	

---

[83]The McKinney-Vento Act requires Education to collect and disseminate certain information regarding homeless children and youth. 42 U.S.C. § 11434(h). Education is required to determine, based on information it collects and information provided by states, the extent to which state educational agencies are ensuring that each homeless child and homeless youth has access to a free appropriate public education. 42 U.S.C. § 11434(f). According to Education, states report data through two methods—on an ongoing basis through its EDFacts database and through the Consolidated State Performance Report, which states must certify annually. The National Center for Homeless Education releases these data in a data collection summary for the EHCY program on an annual basis.

	Grantee districts	Non-grantee districts
Primary nighttime residence by category (sheltered, unsheltered, hotels/motels, and doubled up)	√	√
Academic achievement of homeless students enrolled (reading, mathematics, science)[c]	√	√

Source: Education's Consolidated State Performance Report Federal Data Collection Guide for State Coordinators of Homeless Education School Year 2012-2013. | GAO-14-465

[a]Under the McKinney-Vento Act, students are enrolled if they are "attending classes and participating fully in school activities." 42 U.S.C. § 11434a(1). According to Education, for data collection purposes, an enrolled student includes any child for whom a current enrollment record exists. Children aged 3 through 5 (not kindergarten) includes any preschool-aged (3 through 5) homeless child who is enrolled in a school district-administered preschool program. Children to be included may be attending at a specific location or participating in a home-based program.

[b]For data collection purposes, the definition of served includes homeless children who have been served in any way through McKinney-Vento grant-funded staff or activities. This definition includes children aged birth through 5 years old who are served by the grant program, regardless of whether or not they are enrolled in a preschool program operated by a school district, or in a preschool program where the school district is a partner administratively or financially, or has any accountability in serving the children. It is possible for a child to be served in a district, but not enrolled in that district.

[c]Academic achievement refers to the number of students taking assessment exams and the percentage of students taking the exam that met or exceeded state proficiency standards.

Education has increased the number of data elements it requires school districts, particularly non-grantee districts, to report in the Consolidated State Performance Report. For example, in school year 2010-11, Education began requiring states to report information on the academic achievement of homeless students in reading and mathematics from non-grantee school districts, data that had been required from grantee districts since at least the 2004-05 school year.[84] In school year 2011-12, Education added corresponding data elements in science for all districts to the Consolidated State Performance Report. In school year 2012-13, Education began requiring states to report information on the number of homeless students enrolled in each district, by certain subcategories.[85] Previously, Education had only required states to report this information by subcategory for grantee districts; for non-grantee districts, states were

---

[84]These data included the number and percentage of homeless students who were enrolled in school and assessed in reading and math and the percent of these students who achieved proficiency levels.

[85]The subcategories of homeless children and youth are (1) unaccompanied homeless youth, (2) migratory children and youth, (3) children with disabilities, and (4) Limited English Proficient students.

only required to report the total number of homeless students enrolled and their primary nighttime residence.

Education presents trends in data on homeless students over time in its Consolidated State Performance Report;[86] however, there are limitations to the use of state-reported data to assess the program's results. For example, the state data on the number of homeless students are likely incomplete or unreliable due in part to the under-identification of eligible students. In Education's survey of states, 13 of the 25 states that responded to this question had found that at least one grantee was not in compliance with the statutory requirement to identify homeless children and youth. In one of the four states we reviewed, Education found the data on the number of homeless students to be unreliable, which the state EHCY program coordinator attributed to a 2009-10 transition to a new, state-wide database system that led to undercounting homeless students. Both Education and the state educational agency are taking steps to address the state's data quality issues, according to officials from both agencies. Education officials told us that the under-representation of the number of homeless students in the data generally is an area of concern, which they are addressing in multiple ways. In addition to questioning states about this issue, an Education official said the agency has worked with a contractor who analyzed school district-level data in every state to help identify school districts that may have been under-identifying homeless students by comparing their rate of homeless student identification to the percentage of students receiving free or reduced-price lunch. The contractor has made presentations on the results of this analysis to state EHCY program coordinators, and Education plans to provide state EHCY program coordinators with additional technical assistance on outreach and identification.

---

[86]As of March 2014, Education was not able to calculate percentage changes in enrollment and nighttime residence data from year to year due to a recent change in how it produced these data, but anticipated being able to do so in future years. Beginning in school year 2011-12, Education required states to identify which districts received grants and which did not. As a result, Education was able to report enrollment and primary nighttime residence data by grantees and non-grantees using school district-level data, instead of state-level data. However, because homeless students frequently move from district to district, it is possible that the same student would be reported by multiple districts in a state in the school district-level data. Consequently, increases in enrollment data from year to year may be a result of this duplication as well as to an actual increase in the number of homeless students. See U.S. Department of Education, National Center for Homeless Education, *Education for Homeless Children and Youths Program Data Collection Summary* (March 2014).

Another limitation to the use of state-reported data is that, by design, the data are difficult to compare across states. As GAO has previously reported, states vary in how they measure student academic achievement, as permitted by ESEA, to allow states to address their unique circumstances.[87] Education has acknowledged this inherent limitation, as well as challenges in comparing data within states over time, as many states have made changes to their state assessments that can impact comparability.[88] According to the Common Core State Standards Initiative, a voluntary state-led initiative, 43 states and the District of Columbia have chosen to adopt the Common Core State Standards—designed to define the knowledge and skills students should gain throughout their K-12 education in order to graduate high school prepared to succeed in entry-level careers, introductory academic college courses, and workforce training programs. Most states have chosen to participate in one of two state-led consortia working to develop assessments based on these standards, expected to be available in school year 2014-15, which may lead to greater comparability across states. Similarly, according to agency officials, Education collects dropout and graduation rate data, including disaggregated data for homeless students, but these data are calculated differently in different states—making comparisons across states problematic.[89] GAO has previously reported on the use of different state graduation rates, and recommended that Education provide information to all states on ways to account for different types of students

[87]GAO, *No Child Left Behind Act: Improvements Needed in Education's Process for Tracking States' Implementation of Key Provisions,* GAO-04-734 (Washington, D.C.: Sept. 30, 2004).

[88]Academic achievement data may be particularly unreliable for homeless students, who tend to move frequently and often have erratic school attendance, increasing the likelihood that they will miss taking the academic achievement exams, which are typically given only once during high school.

[89]In addition, school districts have difficulty tracking students who leave school because they do not know whether a student has dropped out of school or is enrolled in another school district, undermining the reliability of the dropout data. Our previous work found that student mobility was the primary factor affecting the accuracy of graduation rates; students who come and go make it difficult to keep accurate records. See GAO, *No Child Left Behind Act: Education Could Do More to Help States Better Define Graduation Rates and Improve Knowledge About Intervention Strategies,* GAO-05-879 (Washington, D.C.: Sept. 20, 2005).

in graduation rate calculations and assess the reliability of state data used to calculate interim rates, which it did.[90]

Aside from its annual data collection efforts, Education's latest study (forthcoming in 2014), which covers school year 2010-11, will provide some valuable information on program implementation, according to agency officials. The study collects information from surveys of state EHCY program coordinators and grantee school district homeless liaisons on topics such as their EHCY-related responsibilities; data collection and use; collaboration with other programs and service providers; barriers homeless students face to enrolling, attending, and succeeding in schools; and state monitoring of districts' compliance with the McKinney-Vento Act, among other topics.[91]

Conclusions

The EHCY program, funded at about $65 million for fiscal year 2014, is intended to remove barriers to educational achievement for homeless students and provide them with access to critical services—such as transportation to school and referrals for health care. Such services are important to help mitigate the range of negative effects experienced by homeless children and youth across an array of measures, including academic achievement and school graduation rates. The program identified more than 1.1 million homeless students in school year 2011-12—students who, had they not been identified, might have faced greater difficulties succeeding in school and preparing to graduate. To increase the program's effectiveness, school districts, states, and the federal government leverage existing resources to ensure that homeless students are identified and their various academic and non-academic needs are met. The EHCY program promotes efforts to leverage resources, in part, by requiring coordination and collaboration among various programs and service providers that also serve homeless students. Collaboration can be particularly important for districts and communities addressing significant increases in homelessness following natural disasters.

[90]See GAO-05-879. According to agency officials, Education requires states and school districts to report a standard 4-year adjusted cohort graduation rate for all students. This rate is comparable across states, but it is not disaggregated for homeless students.

[91]Education had initially intended to survey both grantee and non-grantee school districts but found that the variation in how states implement the program prevented doing so.

Appropriately identifying eligible students, in collaboration with other providers, is key to ensuring that districts provide homeless students with the services they need. However, challenges districts face in identifying students coupled with potential financial disincentives to identify them due to the cost of providing them with services such as transportation, can lead to under-identification, which has several consequences. First, it can result in barriers to homeless students' educational stability and achievement. Homeless children and youth who are not identified may have difficulty getting to and from their school as their nighttime residence changes and may therefore be derailed in their attempts to obtain an education without the assistance available through the EHCY program. Second, under-identification complicates Education's ability to fully assess program results due to concerns about the accuracy and completeness of the data, which it has taken some steps to address. Similarly, under-identification complicates the ability of the U.S. Interagency Council on Homelessness to accurately assess progress toward its goal of ending homelessness for families, youth, and children by 2020.

While it may not be possible to accurately determine the extent to which districts may be under-identifying students—and the extent to which these children and youth may not succeed academically— monitoring states and school districts is imperative to ensure compliance with the requirements of the McKinney-Vento Act, particularly in light of the fact that some states are implementing the program differently than described in their state plans. Without monitoring states through regular reviews of state programs and implementation plans, Education will not have the information it needs to determine whether states are meeting requirements that help provide eligible students with the resources needed to pursue an education.

Recommendation for Agency Action

To help ensure state compliance with the McKinney-Vento Act, Education should develop a monitoring plan to ensure adequate oversight of the EHCY program. This plan could, for example, determine a schedule of states to be monitored and incorporate procedures to assess whether states need to update their state plans.

Agency Comments and Our Evaluation

We provided a draft of this report to the Departments of Education, HHS, and HUD and to USICH for review and comment. Education and USICH provided formal comments that are reproduced in appendices III and IV.

Education, HHS, HUD, and USICH also provided technical comments, which we incorporated as appropriate.

Education agreed that sufficient oversight of EHCY program requirements at the federal, state, and local levels is necessary and that both inter-agency and cross-program collaboration is essential to ensure that the needs of homeless children and youth are addressed. Education noted that although not all state EHCY programs have been monitored in recent years, the department has continued to conduct risk assessments for all states and to provide technical assistance to states and school districts through the EHCY program office and NCHE.

Education concurred with our recommendation that, in order to ensure compliance with the McKinney-Vento Act, the department should develop a monitoring plan to ensure adequate oversight of the EHCY program. Education said that it is currently developing a plan for monitoring for fiscal year 2015 and will increase monitoring for the EHCY program, ensuring that all states identified as "higher risk" in its next round of risk assessments are monitored through document reviews, on-site and remote interviews with state and local educational agency personnel. We encourage Education to continue to consider the length of time since a state was last monitored in its determination of risk and to consider developing a monitoring schedule to help ensure that it has the information it needs to determine whether all states are meeting EHCY program requirements. Education also said that it is making changes to its monitoring protocol, adding questions related to student academic achievement and potential under-identification of homeless students. We support Education's decision to increase its EHCY program monitoring and believe focusing additional attention on the issue of under-identification is particularly important. Without a fuller sense of the extent of under-identification, it is difficult for Education to gauge program results. Lastly, Education indicated that it plans to include the development of a secure website through which states can update their state plans in its next technical assistance contract. Since states may have changed the way they implement the EHCY program since their state plans were originally developed, we encourage Education to take steps to ensure that states that need to update their plans do so.

USICH agreed that monitoring EHCY grantees is important to ensure homeless children and youth are identified. USICH also noted the important role that Education can play in fostering best practices, strategic partnerships, and innovation to address the needs of homeless students. USICH stated that it considers Education and the EHCY program to be critical partners in developing and advancing the work of USICH's goal of ending homelessness among families, children, and youth by 2020.

As agreed with your office, unless you publicly announce its contents earlier, we plan no further distribution of this report until 30 days from its issue date. At that time, we will send copies of this report to the Secretaries of Education, HHS, and HUD, the Executive Director of USICH, relevant congressional committees, and other interested parties. In addition, the report will be made available at no charge on the GAO Web site at http://www.gao.gov.

If you or your staff members have any questions about this report, please contact me at (202) 512- 7215 or Brownke@gao.gov. Contact points for our Offices of Congressional Relations and Public Affairs may be found on the last page of this report. GAO staff who made key contributions to this report are listed in appendix V.

Kay E. Brown

Kay E. Brown, Director
Education, Workforce, and Income Security Issues

Appendix I: Scope and Methodology

We used several approaches to obtain information on how school districts, states, and the Department of Education (Education) implement and oversee the Education for Homeless Children and Youth (EHCY) program. To gather information on how the EHCY program is implemented at the local level, we visited three states—Colorado, New Jersey, and Washington State—and conducted interviews with a fourth state, Texas, by phone. We selected states that represent geographic diversity and were identified by experts, including the National Association for the Education of Homeless Children and Youth (NAEHCY) and other national organizations working on issues related to homelessness, for their experiences in providing education to homeless students. We identified these organizations during the course of our background research. We also considered the number of homeless students states identified in recent years, including any trends, the level of program funding states received, and the delivery structure of early childhood education programs in the state. In addition, we selected states that experienced surges in homelessness due to recent natural disasters—including wildfires, flooding, and a hurricane. Together, these states included about 13 percent of identified homeless students nationwide in school year 2011-12. In each state, we interviewed state officials to obtain information on how they collaborate with other agencies, service providers, and school districts, as well as their monitoring practices. We also met with school district officials. In all, we spoke with representatives from 20 school districts in the four states. We selected school districts, with assistance from state EHCY program coordinators, to represent a mix of urban, suburban, and rural districts, as well as districts that received EHCY program funds (grantees) and those that did not (non-grantees). In one state, we also met with representatives of two regional educational entities that are responsible for providing EHCY-related services to several school districts within their respective regions and receive EHCY program funds to do so. In the states we visited, we also met with school officials at the elementary, middle, and high school levels, and youth that have experienced homelessness, or their families, about their educational experiences (12 youth and three families). Information obtained from these states, school districts, youth, and families is non-generalizable. We also attended the 2012 NAEHCY Conference to obtain further insights into how school districts were implementing the EHCY program and met with five additional state coordinators at that conference to discuss how they collaborated with various stakeholders.

To obtain generalizable and national-level information from states and grantee school districts, we analyzed Education data from two surveys covering school year 2010-11. Education's surveys collected information on services school districts provided to homeless children and youth; state and local collaboration efforts with other Education programs; and how states monitored school districts, including any differences in monitoring among grantee and non-grantee districts. A total of 448 school districts were included in the district-level survey sample, including the 50 largest school districts and a random sample of 401 other school districts (3 districts were removed from the sample after the survey was released because they had merged with other districts). The surveys were conducted electronically, however, in a small number of cases (7 or 8) districts that did not initially respond to the electronic survey were administered the survey over the phone or on paper. The school district-level survey had a weighted response rate of 86 percent (96 percent for the 50 largest districts and 85 percent for the remaining 398 districts).[1] The state survey was sent to all 50 states, the District of Columbia, and the Bureau of Indian Affairs. The Bureau of Indian Affairs did not respond and was later removed from the scope of the survey. One additional state provided incomplete survey answers, leaving 49 states and the District of Columbia as the state survey population. We assessed the reliability of Education's survey data by performing electronic testing of the data elements, reviewing relevant documentation, and interviewing agency officials knowledgeable about the data. We found that the data were sufficiently reliable for the purposes of this report. The responses of each eligible sample member who provided a useable questionnaire were weighted in the analyses to account statistically for all members of the population. We created weights for each survey respondent to account for unequal probabilities of selection and various unit response rates among the survey strata. All estimates obtained from the school district-level survey have margins of error of no greater than six percentage points.

To obtain information on how Education administers the EHCY program, we interviewed Education officials about how the agency monitors states for compliance and collaborates with other federal programs. We also interviewed officials from other federal agencies, including the Departments of Health and Human Services (HHS) and Housing and Urban Development (HUD), as well as the U.S. Interagency Council on

---

[1]To determine the weighted response rate, we used the response rate definition "RR3," as defined by the American Association for Public Opinion Research in "Standard Definitions: Final Dispositions of Case Codes and Outcome Rates for Surveys," (Revised 2011). RR3 estimates the proportion of cases of unknown eligibility that are, in fact, eligible.

Homelessness (USICH), to obtain their perspectives on collaborating with Education on programs that serve homeless children and youth. We also interviewed Education officials about the agency's monitoring efforts. Additionally, we reviewed relevant documents—including federal laws and regulations, monitoring protocols, and policy memos—and examined Education's findings on homeless education from state monitoring reports.

We conducted this performance audit from July 2012 through July 2014 in accordance with generally accepted government auditing standards. Those standards require that we plan and perform the audit to obtain sufficient, appropriate evidence to provide a reasonable basis for our findings and conclusions based on our audit objectives. We believe that the evidence obtained provides a reasonable basis for our findings and conclusions based on our audit objectives.

Appendix II: Education for Homeless Children and Youth Program Monitoring Indicators

Federal monitoring indicator	Selected examples of acceptable evidence that states provide
1.1: The state conducts monitoring and evaluation of school districts with and without subgrants, sufficient to ensure compliance with McKinney-Vento program requirements.	Written procedure for monitoring school districts with and without subgrants to include: • Recent copy of monitoring policies and procedures, schedules for current and previous school years. • Sample notification letters to school districts, preparation checklists, or other forms. • A copy of the interview protocol for school district reviews. • Most recent copies of reports, recommendations and follow-up to corrective actions.
2.1: The state implements procedures to address the identification, enrollment and retention of homeless students through coordinating and collaborating with other program offices and state agencies.	Written communication to school districts updating state policies and procedures that address the problems homeless children and youth face in school enrollment and retention since the last Department of Education program review. Updates to the state plan, including the completion of planned activities and proposals for new state-level activities.
2.2: The state provides, or provides for, technical assistance to school districts to ensure appropriate implementation of the statute.	Copies of written guidance to school districts and/or information dissemination materials distributed electronically or by other means. The most recent liaison orientation, on-line trainings, conferences, and regional training agendas and technical assistant log.
3.1 The state ensures that school district subgrant plans for services to eligible homeless students meet all requirements.	Evidence that the state has an application and approval process to provide competitive subgrants to school districts.
3.2: The state complies with the statutory and other regulatory requirements governing the reservation of funds for state-level coordination activities.	State budget detail on reserved funds for state-level coordination activities for the current fiscal year and use of funds for the last fiscal year.
3.3: The state has a system for ensuring the prompt resolution of disputes.	Updated state dispute resolution policy and procedures including: • procedures for tracking disputes • documents indicating that dispute procedures have been implemented • records indicating that disputes are addressed, investigated and resolved in a timely manner Evidence that the state tracks if school districts have a dispute resolution policy in place.

Source: Department of Education. | GAO-14-465

Appendix III: Comments from the Department of Education

UNITED STATES DEPARTMENT OF EDUCATION

OFFICE OF ELEMENTARY AND SECONDARY EDUCATION

WASHINGTON, D.C. 20202

THE ASSISTANT SECRETARY

July 18, 2014

Ms. Kay E. Brown
Director
Education, Workforce, and Income Security Issues
Government Accountability Office
441 G Street, NW
Washington, DC 20548

Dear Ms. Brown:

I am writing in response to the recommendation made in the Government Accountability Office's (GAO's) draft report, "Education of Homeless Students: Improved Program Oversight Needed" (GAO-14-465). I appreciate the opportunity to comment on the draft report on behalf of the U.S. Department of Education (Department).

We appreciate GAO's comprehensive review of how the Federal government, State educational agencies, and school districts are addressing the requirements of the Education for Homeless Children and Youth (EHCY) program authorized under Title VII-B of the McKinney-Vento Homeless Assistance Act, as well as the inter- and intra-agency coordination of programs serving homeless children and youth. The Department shares the view, outlined in the report, that given the increasing numbers of students identified as experiencing homelessness by our nation's public schools in recent years and complex demands for coordination of services, there needs to be sufficient oversight of requirements at the Federal, State, and local levels. We also agree that inter-agency and cross-program collaboration is critical to addressing the needs of homeless children and youth, particularly with respect to natural disaster assistance, early childhood education, and coordination with housing and human service programs serving children and youth experiencing homelessness.

The Department acknowledges that since transitioning to a risk assessment-based protocol for monitoring, not every State has been monitored in recent years. Though this change resulted in a decrease in the number of States monitored annually, the Department has not only continued to conduct risk assessments of all 50 States, it either maintained or increased activities designed to support State and local efforts related to program administration and improving the education of homeless students, including regular, high-quality technical assistance to States and school districts provided by the EHCY program office and its contractor for the National Center for Homeless Education. To these points, we appreciate that GAO's report makes mention of the Department's more recent efforts

www.ed.gov

400 MARYLAND AVE., SW, WASHINGTON, DC 20202

The Department of Education's mission is to promote student achievement and preparation for global competitiveness by fostering educational excellence and ensuring equal access.

with respect to homeless education. In particular, the Department has played a significant role in recent Federal interagency efforts to address homelessness, and we are committed to continuing our involvement in these efforts. The Department also has made strides in collecting, using, and disseminating data regarding students experiencing homelessness through the annual Consolidated State Performance Report and ED*Facts* Reporting System.

The report offered one recommendation for agency action –

Recommendation: *To help ensure state compliance with the McKinney-Vento Act, Education should develop a monitoring plan to ensure adequate oversight of the EHCY program. This plan could, for example, determine a schedule of states to be monitored and incorporate procedures to assess whether states need to update their state plans.*

Response: The Department understands that adequate oversight of the EHCY program is critically important to the success of homeless students. We are currently developing a plan for monitoring for the 2015 fiscal year and will increase monitoring for the EHCY program. Following the next round of risk assessments, the Department plans to monitor any State identified as "higher risk" and will budget for sufficient capacity to monitor effectively, including document reviews, on-site and remote interviews with SEA and local agency personnel with EHCY-related duties, notification of findings and/or recommendations, and instituting corrective action measures as necessary. Further, owing to our recently enhanced capacity to use data from LEAs, a new monitoring protocol will include questions about the academic performance and potential under-identification of homeless students in all LEAs in a State. We believe our enhanced protocol and new monitoring plan will translate into strengthened oversight of the EHCY program. Lastly, our next contract for a national homeless education technical assistance center, to be awarded in September 2014, will include the development of a secure extranet Web site through which States can update their State plans more regularly and in ways that State Coordinators have identified as being meaningful for program administration.

We appreciate the opportunity to review the draft report and comment on the recommendations. I am also enclosing a document with technical comments.

Sincerely,

Deborah S. Delisle

Enclosure

2

Appendix IV: Comments from the U.S. Interagency Council on Homelessness

July 22, 2014

Ms. Kay E. Brown, Director
Education, Workforce, and Income Security Issues
U.S. Government Accountability Office
441 G Street, NW
Washington, DC 20548

Dear Ms. Brown:

The U.S. Interagency Council on Homelessness (USICH) appreciates the opportunity to comment on the Government Accountability Office (GAO) July 2014 draft report *Education of Homeless Students: Improved Program Oversight Needed* (GAO-14-465). USICH's close collaboration with the Department of Education (ED) and other Council agencies informs our response to the report and its recommendations.

We appreciate GAO's attention to the challenges involved in consistently identifying and connecting students experiencing homelessness with appropriate interventions. We share the urgency conveyed in the report to address homelessness among students and all Americans, which is enshrined in the goals of *Opening Doors*. Specifically, the Obama Administration has committed to end homelessness for families, children, and youth—including students experiencing homelessness—by 2020. The Administration views homelessness among children and youth as an urgent crisis and concurs that homelessness for students can have negative impacts on their ability to access and take full advantage of educational opportunities.

USICH is working with ED and other Council agencies to achieve our goal of ending homelessness among families, children, and youth by 2020. Through two interagency working groups—one on families with children and another on youth—Council member agencies are implementing strategies to increase community capacity to identify homelessness and connect families and youth to stable housing and supports to improve health, employment, and educational outcomes. ED and the EHCY program are critical partners in developing and advancing this work.

The central insight motivating strategies for ending homelessness among families with children and youth is that we must scale up the interventions known to work, based on data and research. ED's partnership with USICH and other Council agencies is focused primarily on helping to identify the collaborations at a local level that can support better linkages between schools and other parts of the homeless response system, which in turn improves housing and educational outcomes for students experiencing homelessness and their families. To this end, ED and USICH developed comprehensive strategies to improve collaboration between schools and homeless services organizations. Use of data is a central theme of this effort, spotlighting local partnerships that use data on homelessness among students from schools to inform the planning of the community's response to youth homelessness.

The focus of GAO's report calls attention to the important role ED plays in monitoring activities for EHCY grantees. USICH agrees that monitoring is important in identifying children and youth experiencing homelessness. At the same time, focusing exclusively or primarily on this role could inadvertently overlook the equally important role that ED can play in fostering local school and homeless services partnerships. While monitoring can be vital, particularly where practice diverges from requirements or fails to achieve core purposes, we advise GAO consider a more expansive view of the role ED can play not only in ensuring *compliance,* but also in fostering best practices, strategic partnerships, and innovation. We believe the central focus of ED's activities under EHCY is advancing practice by supporting such innovation.

To achieve both roles, ED needs adequate resources and staff capacity. The current scale of resources and staffing allocated to EHCY presents a challenge to ED's ability to adequately monitor EHCY grantees and foster best practices at the local level. The $65 million allocated to the program dispersed among the 1,168,354 million students identified in schools as homeless equates to only $55.63 dollars per student per year. USICH and the Administration recognize that additional resources are needed to end homelessness among families and youth and stand as a committed partner to Congress and leaders in communities across the country in developing a more robust response to the crisis facing far too many young people.

Thank you for the opportunity to comment on this report.

Sincerely,

Laura Green Zeilinger
Executive Director

2

Appendix V: GAO Contact and Staff Acknowledgments

GAO Contact	Kay E. Brown, (202) 512-7215 or brownke@gao.gov
Staff Acknowledgments	In addition to the contact named above, Kathryn Larin (Assistant Director), Avani Locke (Analyst-in-Charge), David Barish, and Jennifer Cook made key contributions to this report. Also contributing to this report were Alicia Cackley, Sarah Cornetto, Keira Dembowski, Justin Fisher, Hedieh Fusfield, Jessica Gray, Thomas James, Jean McSween, Mimi Nguyen, Paul Schmidt, Almeta Spencer, Kathleen van Gelder, and Amber Yancey-Carroll.

Related GAO Products

Managing for Results: Implementation Approaches Used to Enhance Collaboration in Interagency Groups. GAO-14-220. Washington, D.C.: February 14, 2014.

Homelessness: Fragmentation and Overlap in Programs Highlight the Need to Identify, Assess, and Reduce Inefficiencies. GAO-12-491. Washington, D.C.: May 10, 2012.

Homelessness: To Improve Data and Programs, Agencies Have Taken Steps to Develop a Common Vocabulary. GAO-12-302T. Washington, D.C.: December 15, 2011.

K-12 Education: Many Challenges Arise in Educating Students Who Change Schools Frequently. GAO-11-40. Washington, D.C.: November 18, 2010.

Homelessness: A Common Vocabulary Could Help Agencies Collaborate and Collect More Consistent Data. GAO-10-702. Washington, D.C.: June 30, 2010.

Runaway and Homeless Youth Grants: Improvements Needed in the Grant Award Process. GAO-10-335. Washington, D.C.: May 10, 2010.

Disconnected Youth: Federal Action Could Address Some of the Challenges Faced by Local Programs That Reconnect Youth to Education and Employment. GAO-08-313. Washington, D.C.: February 28, 2008.